D0409474

THE REALITY OF ORGANIZATIONS

The Reality of Organizations

A Guide for Managers

Third Edition

Rosemary Stewart

150th YEAR

MACMILLAN

First published 1970 by
THE MACMILLAN PRESS LTD
Houndmills, Basingstoke, Hampshire RG21 2XS
and London
Companies and representatives
throughout the world

ISBN 0–333–59550–5 hardcover
ISBN 0–333–59551–3 paperback

A catalogue record for this book is available
from the British Library.

Printed in Great Britain by
Mackays of Chatham PLC
Chatham, Kent

Second edition 1985
Third edition 1993
Reprinted 1994

Contents

I dedicate this book gratefully to the many managers, in companies and the public sector, who have willingly contributed their understanding of management to research projects and shared their problems in discussions over the years. I hope that it may be of help to all those who want to learn more about organizing effectively.

Introduction to the Third Edition

Managers are busy people. Is the study of organization sufficiently useful to be worth the time that it will take? This question is one that any teacher of, or writer on, the subject ought to answer. It is not so obviously useful a study as that of finance, or marketing, yet many managers have organizational problems as well as financial and marketing ones. Can they be helped by learning more about the subject? This book is written in the belief that they can, based on the experience of discussing organizational problems with very diverse groups of managers.

Small organizations can work well with little formal structure, but as they become larger more attention needs to be given to organization; enthusiasm, flair and drive are no longer sufficient. Creative chaos, the enthusiastic pursuit of new ideas with the maximum of flexibility and little planning and coordination becomes progressively more costly as different activities get out of step. There comes a time, therefore, in the growth of a company when more thought needs to be given to how work and relationships should be organized.

Managers in larger organizations may be forced to think about organization because of the complexities inherent in trying to get a large number of people to work together for common objectives. Most of them will, at times, be only too well aware of organizational deficiencies: of work that does not get done; of conflicts between departments; of failures in communication up and down the hierarchy; and of the difficulties of knowing what is happening in other parts of the group.

Managers can learn to recognize when they should be thinking about organization. They can learn to know when they have a problem which is, at least in part, an organizational one, and can learn to diagnose what kind of problem it is. They can also get some help in deciding what to do about it, although at the present state of our knowledge they can usually get more help in diagnosis than in prescription.

There is rarely a solution to an organizational problem that does not create fresh difficulties. Usually it is a question of finding the best balance between the advantages and disadvantages of different forms of organization. Only occasionally is there a clear-cut answer that is obviously preferable. The study of organization is, therefore, primarily useful as a means of achieving a greater understanding of the types of problems that can arise, their causes, and their symptoms. It can also provide guides to coping with problems but no clear answers to them.

The success of the form of organization must be judged by the extent to which it helps the achievement of common objectives. A good organization is one that does so as efficiently as possible. This book does not describe the process of defining objectives since this has so often been done elsewhere, but readers should remember that a review of organizational effectiveness must start with a definition of objectives for each of the main areas of the business or service.

Since *The Reality of Organizations* was first written in 1970 many other books about organizations and organizing have been published. Yet this book has continued to sell for over 20 years: hence this third edition. New readers, however, need an answer to the question: 'What is different about this book?' and more importantly: 'How can it help me to understand better how organizations work and so to be more effective as a manager?' Readers who have used an earlier edition of this book for their students need to know what has been changed in this new edition.

Books about organization are of four different kinds: one, textbooks, that are often lengthy – particularly if they are American – written solely for students; two, at the opposite end, are the recipe books written for managers with no information about cooking ingredients or the processes of cooking – the tips, lists and guidelines group which say what to do, but not why or in what conditions it is likely to work. In between these two extremes are books addressed to managers, whether as students or not, that also seek to be of practical help but consider that an understanding of the nature of the problem is the first and essential step to trying to solve it. They aim to help managers to understand the tasks of organizing, and how and why difficulties arise, before offering any advice on how to reduce organizational problems. This book belongs in that third group. It will draw upon the fourth group, which are reports of the findings of particular organizational studies, for what they can tell us about the problems of organizing and how to reduce them.

The Reality of Organizations is addressed to managers and professional staff, whether in industry, commerce, the public sector or voluntary organizations. Each may tend to think of their problems as special. Yet there are many common problems as will be shown by the examples.

The advantage of writing a new edition of a longstanding book, rather than starting afresh, is that it provides a perspective on what has changed in organizations, what is changing and what problems remain the same. It encourages drawing upon writers over a long time span because some of the earlier writers illuminated well problems that are perennial or provided what was then a new perspective that still proves of value.

The focus of this book is upon the tasks and problems of organizing in a changing world; the choices to be made and their advantages and disadvantages. It stresses that the aim should be to find the right balance between these for the current situation, but to be aware of the trade-offs that have to be made. These are not fashionable topics, like leadership (about which the author has written elsewhere[1]), but they are still an essential aspect of understanding how to organize effectively. Organizations are complex and difficult to manage well, hence the warning against the dangers of fashions in organizing, of believing that the latest technique for enlisting commitment and improving organizational effectiveness is a panacea.

This book was originally written as a companion to *The Reality of Management*, which has had an even longer life than this one. It continues, while its successor, *Managing Today and Tomorrow*,[2] takes a broader view of the tasks and problems of managing and of how these are changing.

The previous edition of *The Reality of Organizations* was published in 1985. Since then there have been major changes affecting organizations in the public and the private sector of which this new edition must take account. These changes have made managers' lives harder, but most of them are intensifications of previous changes: greater and more global competition; the development of the European Community and new technical changes, including major changes in computing and related technologies. Changes in the public sector, particularly but by no means solely in Britain, have been even greater than in companies.

The structure of the book, which was designed for easy reading, and the individual chapters remain the same but the content is often revised substantially – about a third of the book has been rewritten – to take account of changes in organizations and in their environment. New sections are added to discuss these changes. Elsewhere the emphasis and the examples given are often changed. The lengthy examples of how external changes have affected particular organizations are updated: the original choice of ICL as an example of the changes affecting a company over time continues to provide a vivid example of the extent of external and internal changes. The main changes to the book are from Chapter 6 on.

This book is designed to be read either as a whole or for individual chapters. Summaries at the end of each chapter are there to help the readers decide whether it is one that they want to read in full. The last chapter summarizes what has gone before by describing some of the most common mistakes. The aim throughout is to help managers to understand their organizational problems and to know what are the advantages and disadvantages of different ways of dealing with them.

NOTES

1. Rosemary Stewart, *Leading in the NHS: A Practical Guide* (London: Macmillan, 1989).
2. Rosemary Stewart, *Managing Today and Tomorrow* (London: Macmillan, 1991).

Part I
Theory

Many managers are unsympathetic, even antagonistic, to theoretical writing on management. Since this book is addressed to managers, Part I is the shortest. It could not be omitted, because a manager's understanding of organizational problems will be increased by the framework for thinking about organization which the different theories provide. The single chapter that makes up Part I describes how different theorists have looked at organizations and what they have contributed that can be useful to the manager.

1 Ways of Looking at Organizations

INTRODUCTION

This book is about practice rather than theory; about the problems that arise in organizing and about what can be said about them that could be useful to the practising manager. However, even the most practical managers can think about a problem more easily if they have some frame of reference that will help them to decide what kind of problem it is. Like the physician looking at a patient, they need to diagnose the class of malady. It may be a defect in the circulation system, when knowledge of its working and of the imbalance to which it is subject would be useful; or it may be a digestive problem, in which case a different area of knowledge would be appropriate. They might even decide that the malady is both a circulatory and a digestive one. Admittedly, knowledge of how the human body works is much more advanced than our understanding of the working of human organizations. Even so, theories of organization can give the manager greater insight into the nature of organizational problems.

Organizations are highly complex. We do not understand enough about how they work to have developed comprehensive theories. Instead we have a number of partial explanations which have been put forward by writers from different backgrounds. Each represents a different way of looking at organizations. An understanding of these different viewpoints can help managers to identify what kind of problem they are worrying about. Each of these schools of thought has made a contribution to our understanding of the way organizations work, but each also has its limitations – often not sufficiently appreciated by their supporters. This chapter will examine briefly the uses and limitations of three ways of looking at organizations, and then illustrate how all could be helpful in tackling a particular problem. These three are the main, but not the only, ways of looking at organizations, as Gareth Morgan has shown in his account of eight different images of organizations.[1]

THE CLASSICAL SCHOOL

The earliest writers on organization, like many managers today, thought of it as a formal structure. They sought to describe the rules – called principles – which should be used in designing this structure. Such principles were, they thought, applicable to all types of formal organization. These writers – called the classical school – and their successors discussed how to plan the formal organization of work.[2] They were concerned with the best way of dividing up the tasks to be done, with how to group these together into departments, and with how to deal with the problems of coordination. They paid particular attention to organizational relationships between line and staff. They stressed the need for a clear definition of responsibilities and of authority. Their chief contribution is the definition of responsibilities and of the tasks that have to be considered in building up an organization. They provided a frame of reference that will help any manager to think clearly about the nature of the work to be done, about the best ways of dividing it up into jobs and departments and then of how to coordinate these divisions.

The work of these classical writers is not by itself sufficient for an understanding of organization; its approach has important limitations. It is too concerned with the formal structure, not sufficiently with the individuals who make the structure work. It is a static approach, emphasizing hierarchy and paying too little attention to the many interactions that take place between different parts of an organization. It emphasizes similarities, without giving sufficient attention to the diversity of problems met in different types of organization. It stemmed from manufacturing, particularly mass production, and ignored the requirements of other kinds of organizations. The classical approach, then, has a particular viewpoint which has both virtues and limitations. The virtues remain although they are less useful in a world where organizations are changing frequently. The limitations have been compensated for by other ways of looking at organizations, which will be described next.

PEOPLE IN ORGANIZATIONS

The classical writers thought of organization as a formal structure. Another way of thinking about it, and one which all managers use, is in terms of the people who are employed within it. Managers cannot think solely of boxes on charts or of job descriptions; they have also to think of how Tom, Mary and Bill will get on if Bill is selected for the vacant job. When a man or woman is being recruited from outside, the selectors will often ask themselves 'Is this candidate likely to be acceptable to his or her colleagues?'

Managers, then, are usually sensitive to the fact that how well staff work together may affect how well the organization works – though they may forget that this is also true of those lower down the hierarchy with whom they have little or no personal contact. They may go further and try to understand *why* people behave as they do and *what* influences their behaviour. This is where the second group of writers can be useful in helping the manager to think analytically about people's behaviour.

Interest in how people behave in organizations dates from the famous Hawthorne studies into the effects of fatigue on workers' productivity. These were carried out at the Western Electric Company in Chicago in the 1920s by Elton Mayo and others.[3] One study observed the effects of introducing rest periods of different frequency and length. The remarkable thing about this was that throughout the period of the experiment, which lasted several years, the output of the small group of girls being studied increased– apart from some minor fluctuations – whatever changes were made, including one change when rest periods were abolished. The conclusions drawn from this and other research in the works was that the sense of belonging to a work group and the nature of first–line supervision were both important factors in morale. The Hawthorne studies, and many subsequent ones, have shown that the way people behave at work is affected by many other factors than the nature of the economic incentives that they are offered.

The second main group of writers on organization stem from the Hawthorne studies. They are called the human relations or the behavioural school.[4] These writers look at organizations as composed both of individuals, with different needs that can be studied, and of groups of people who develop their own ways of doing things and their own codes of conduct. Unlike the classical school, they are research-orientated. They try to find out what happens before seeking to explain it.

This approach to the study of organizations has also contributed much that can be of value to managers who want to understand why apparently sensible and logical plans are often frustrated. If they look at a job only from the classical point of view they will think of the tasks that have to be done, but not of what it is like for the person who has to do them. An understanding of the latter is one guide to why a person in that job may behave in a particular way. Managers need to be sensitive to the kind of strains that may be imposed on the occupants of certain jobs.

A classic study of job stress came from research into human relations in some American restaurants. The study could be subtitled 'Why waitresses weep', for it showed that in some restaurants the waitresses quite often cried.

The explanation was not that these restaurants had unluckily recruited girls who were lachrymose but that, as the restaurant was organized, the waitresses found themselves in a position of stress. The customers clamoured impatiently for their food, but the waitresses could not satisfy their demands until the counterhand gave them their order. He did not like the waitresses being able to tell him what to do, so he made them wait for their orders. He could then feel that he was boss, instead of being bossed by them.[5]

The illustration above is only one of many studies that have shown how the method of organization can affect people's behaviour. This finding should be remembered by managers who are worrying about the way some of their staff are behaving. They should ask themselves 'What are they reacting to?', 'Is the form of organization to blame?' and, if so, 'Would a different arrangement make people work better?' Quite simple changes may improve relationships. For example, in one of the restaurants studied the waitresses wrote out order slips and put them on a prong. The counterhand could then decide how to fill them without feeling that the waitresses were ordering him about; tension between the two was reduced. Sometimes there may be nothing managers can do to make the job less stressful. Even then it is useful for them to understand what is the cause of the trouble, so that they will not fool themselves by thinking that if the individual in the job is changed the problem will disappear. An awareness of the stressfulness of certain jobs can be equally useful when recruiting, as some people react less to stress than others.

The effects can also flow the other way, from people to organization. Employees can, and do, modify the formal organization. Individual develop their own ways of doing things and groups form their own codes of conduct which are different from those officially prescribed. The manager needs to be conscious of how far what actually happens may differ from what is supposed to happen. What can be called the informal organization may make for efficiency, as passengers by air or train realize all too keenly when industrial action takes the form of working to rule. For example, the official procedures may be unrealistically restrictive; they may never have been the best way to get things done, or conditions may have changed so that they have become inappropriate. Whatever the reason, it may often be more efficient for staff to devise their own methods of getting things done instead of keeping to the official ways. This is an argument for reviewing the formal organization at intervals to see if it needs altering to meet changed circumstances. People are ingenious in making organizations work, but they will work better with an appropriate formal organization. A large gap between what is prescribed in formal organizational policies and procedures and what happens in practice may also be an argument for having a less bureaucratic organization. This argument is strongest when what needs doing cannot be prescribed in advance.

The informal organization may be furthering the objectives of the concern more effectively than the formal, but it can also be in conflict with them. Employees may develop their own ways of doing things to further their own ends, not the organization's. They may, as research has shown, cheat, cover up errors, restrict output, or just arrange to have an easier life. No manager should be so naive as to believe that plans are necessarily carried out in the way prescribed. The research findings of the human relations school can help the manager to be more aware of what is actually happening.

The human relations school provides a different approach to organizational problems from that of the classical writers, but it also has its limitations. Some of its supporters have claimed too much for what can be achieved by thinking about people's needs and behaviour. A bigger limitation is that, although we have learnt a lot about people in organizations, there is still much that we do not understand about human behaviour. We have learnt that it is not only much more complex than the idea of economic man (one whose dominant motivation is the desire for wealth), but also more complex than the early human relations writers realized. The effects of morale on productivity, for example, have been shown to be more elusive than was first thought – a depressing discovery for those who believed that making the workers happy would necessarily result in high productivity.

The human relations school has also applied its research approach to the study of organizational structures. The classical school had theorized about what is the right structure. Social scientists have studied what types of organization exist in practice. These studies have shown that what is a suitable form of organization for one kind of activity will not be for another. There is not, as the classical writers believed, one best form of organization. What is appropriate depends upon many different variables, such as the size of the organization, the rate of change affecting it and its technology. Unfortunately, as studies of what variables affect the design of organizations (called contingency theory) have developed the lessons for managers have become less clear. Probably the most useful is that the greater the uncertainty the more top management will have to give operational management discretion to decide what to do.[6]

SYSTEMS APPROACH TO ORGANIZATION

It is now unusual to pick up a book on management or on organization without seeing the word 'system'. We read of the systems approach, of social systems, socio–technical systems and of systems analysis. The word 'system' has a long lineage in the physical sciences. It can be defined, as in *Webster's Seventh New Collegiate Dictionary*, as 'a regularly interacting or interdependent group of items forming a unified whole'.

What does the use of the word 'system' tell us about our organization that we did not know before? Sometimes the answer is nothing. It may only be used as a buzz word which is tacked on to others indiscriminately, yet when this fashionable froth is ignored we are left with insights into management and organization that are worthy of the manager's attention. The value of looking at an organization from the systems approach is that it changes one's viewpoint from the description and analysis of its component parts to that of their interrelationships. Such an approach emphasizes that one should not try and deal with problems in isolation but should be aware of their interactions.

We are familiar with mechanical systems such as that of our central heating or car. We know that our car is made up of a number of subsystems, and that it is useful to know which system is likely to be responsible for our breakdown. We may find it harder to think of our organization as a system, however, though it is probably only the word that bothers us; if we think, as we should, of the organization as being made up of interlocking and interacting parts, then the link will be clearer.

Under the heading of 'systems' it is useful to distinguish two different ways of looking at organizations. The first is one that has come to be adopted by many social scientists, and can therefore be called the 'social systems' approach. It is concerned with the interactions between the different aspects of the organization – people, technology and formal structure and between the organization and its environment.[7] The second looks at the organization in terms of the information that is needed for decision-making and coordination, tracing the flow of information through decision centres. It can be called the 'information systems' approach and has its origins in operational research and information technology. It is concerned with information of a formal nature rather than the informal information that circulates via the grapevine.

Social Systems

This view of an organization, as made up of interacting variables, has been used by social scientists as the basis for a variety of studies. The original studies were made by researchers at the Tavistock Institute of Human Relations. They devoted much of their attention to investigating the effects of different forms of technical organization of work on the behaviour of individuals and groups. They found that the method of organizing work affected the way employees behaved, and hence their productivity.

The systems approach has taught us the importance of the concept of boundaries. To describe anything as a system involves describing its boundaries. What the boundaries are and, hence, which system should be studied, depends upon the purpose of one's investigation. What, for example, are the boundaries of the organization? Silly question? We all know what they are: the physical boundaries of plant, buildings and land, the people employed and the capital used. But the organization also exists within the wider systems of its community, of the government and of the country, all of which may affect it. In other words, it is part of a larger system with which it interacts. Deciding what is the appropriate boundary for a particular study tells one what to include in one's study and what to exclude. Are customers, for example, whether they be patients in a hospital or shoppers in a store, part of the organization or not? The answer will depend upon the purpose of the investigation. For example, a large chain store conducted an attitude survey to find out about its employees' morale and the sources of dissatisfaction. It asked its staff what they thought of the wages and conditions of work. The staff thought that they compared favourably with those of other stores. 'How do you like your fellow shop assistants?' – 'They are a friendly group.' 'What do you think of your supervisor?' Again the reply was favourable. The staff liked everything about working for the store, with one most important exception. They did *not* like the customers. This finding show how necessary it was to include the customers within the boundaries of the system to be studied when considering staff morale.

The systems approach changes the way of thinking about an organization. The analogy is no longer a rocky island in calm waters which is unchanged by the sea around it – or in systems terminology, it is not a closed system. It is affected by what happens outside it and also affects the people, organizations and physical environment with which it is in contact across its boundary.

The awareness of boundaries between different systems has led to studies by social scientists of what happens at the interface, that is, where the two systems meet. These have shown that jobs that are located wholly within one system subject their holders to much less stress than those that are at the boundaries between the systems. This is true both of jobs that involve crossing departmental boundaries and of those that involve dealing with people outside the organization. Salesmen, for example, are on the boundary between the organization and its outside environment; their job can be a stressful one because they have to try and reconcile the expectations of the employers with those of the customers with whom they may be in more frequent personal contact. This kind of stress is a feature of many more jobs than before, so managers have to become skilled at managing those who work across the boundary of the organization.

Information Systems

The systems approach applied to information stems from the use of operational research on business problems. In The Second World War operational research was found to be a useful tool. After the War its practitioners began to apply their mathematical techniques to business problems. This involved quantifying the information used in the models of business problems that operational research workers construct. Their approach, and that of systems designers today, emphasizes the importance of information, the usefulness of the models depending upon the relevance and reliability of the information that is employed. The manager is seen as someone who takes decisions on the basis of the information available. The efficiency of management can, therefore, be improved by providing more reliable and up-to-date information and by developing techniques for analysing it.

An organization can be looked at as a mechanism for processing information. The flow of information can be studied to see what routes it travels and whether these are the most appropriate. It can be studied, too, to see at what points on the route decisions have to be taken. A manager can be thought of as a decision centre who can be overloaded by the amount of information and requests for information, just as an electrical switch may be overloaded. Modern computer facilities can reduce this problem by providing access to information in different ways. These facilities mean that managers need to remember less, although they also make the manager potentially more overloaded because so much more information is available for complex decision-making. Increasingly managers need to understand how to make the best use of computers to get the information they need. Often more difficult is to recognize what information could be useful and why.[8]

One of the advantages of looking at an organization as an information system is that it treats information as a management resource and highlights its importance. It also treats it as something that can be studied, like any other system. The danger is that too much importance will be attached to formal information so that the value of informal information and contacts will not be appreciated. There may also be too much emphasis on managers as decision-makers and not enough on their task of maintaining existing operations and of encouraging commitment.

USING THE THREE APPROACHES

The systems approach in all its forms has also contributed to our understanding of how organizations work. It is another way of looking at them
and one that can fruitfully be combined with the two other approaches. Its
chief merit is that it focuses attention on the interrelationships between
different aspects of an organization and between the organization and its
environment. ('Environment' is used here to mean everything outside the
organization that can affect it.) The systems viewpoint also has its limitations, however. A study of the relationships between systems does not do
away with the need to examine the component parts. An organization cannot be seen simply as an information system, as some enthusiasts appear
to suggest. It is helpful to use the different tools available for exploring
and analysing decision alternatives, but we must not do that at the expense
of ignoring the way in which people may affect the most orderly plans.

All these ways of looking at organizations – the classical, the human
relations and the systems – can be of help to the manager. One or two of
them may be the most useful at a particular time; often an awareness of all
of them will be desirable. What each has to contribute can be illustrated by
looking at the way in which their supporters might tackle a particular
problem.

Let us take a common problem in large organizations, that of relations
between the managers, who are in charge of the local units, and the head
office. This problem occurs in many different organizations, for example,
manufacturing companies with a number of different works, retail chain
stores, some governmental departments, the health service and in many
charities. What could each of the three ways of looking at organizations
contribute to reducing the problem? For example, a construction company
asks a consultant who uses the classical approach, a social scientist using
the human relations approach but who is also familiar with social systems
thinking, and a consultant with a background in systems design to look at
the following problem and to make recommendations to improve it. Each
of these consultants is told that managers at head office complain that they
do not have adequate information about what is happening on the site. The
site agents, who are the managers in charge of an individual site, complain
that 'they' at head office make demands that do not take into account local
problems, and that the services provided by central service departments are
not available quickly enough when they need them. The site agents also
complain of interference by head office specialists who are out of touch
with local conditions.

✷ The consultant with the classical approach starts by asking a variety of questions to find out whether the duties of particular jobs, and the relationships between them, are well defined. Has the site agent a clear definition of the responsibilities of the job, including responsibilities for reporting to head office? Do site agents know what are the objectives that they should be aiming at? Are the relations between the site agent and specialist departments at head office clearly defined? Do both know when specialists have functional authority; that is, when they can say what must be done, as distinct from when they can merely advise? Who do the site agents reports to? Is there a clear line of authority? How many people report to their boss? Is it too many for the exercise of adequate supervision? The classical approach, therefore, would be to look for one source of the difficulties in a failure to clarify responsibilities and authority.

✷ The social scientist starts by trying to find out what the job of the site agent is like, what demands it makes and what strains and stresses it imposes. She asks the site agents how they see their role; that is, the part they should play. She asks, too, what they think head office expects them to do and what they expect of head office. Their boss at head office, and the other people they have contact with, are also asked what they expect of the site agents. The social scientist then compares these different expectations to see if they agree. If not, this could be indicative of a conflict or confusion between the job of the site agent as seen by the jobholders and that as seen by head office.

Next, this consultant looks at the nature of the contacts that exist between the site agent and managers at head office. How much personal contact is there between them? Do people from head office come down to the site to see conditions for themselves and to discuss them on the spot? How good an understanding do people at head office have of the problems that the site agent has to deal with? What things do site agents think the head office should and should not be told?

The social scientist might also use the systems approach to analyse the site agent's job. She would think of the different systems that are relevant to the problem of the relationships between the site agents and head office. Site agents are on the boundary between head office and the site and likely to be faced with conflicts between the expectations of the two groups. They are also on the boundary between their company and the client's organization; again, there may be conflicts between their expectations. She would describe what these conflicts are and what effect they have on the site agent's actions.

The recommendation of the social scientist might be to provide opportunities for head office staff to have a better understanding of the problems met by the site agent. Like the classical approach, the human relations approach might also stress the need for both groups to be clear about what the objectives of the site agent should be and how these should be related to the objectives of the company as a whole.

The consultant with a background in systems design would look at the nature and flow of information between head office and the site. What kind of information goes from the site to head office? Who receives it there and what happens to it? He would also look at the information-flow from head office to the site. He would be interested both in the content of the information and in the channels that it passes through. He might find out that some people who should be receiving certain information are not doing so and that others are receiving redundant information. He might also discover that unfavourable information from the site is being delayed because the site agent hopes that things will get better (a discovery that the social scientist might also have made when interviewing the site agent). The systems analyst would try to find out what information is needed by the site agent and at head office and compare this with the information that they are currently getting. His recommendation might be to reassess what information is needed at head office, and by whom.

Top management would receive the recommendations of the three advisers, recommendations which might have little or no overlap. They might express surprise at the differences in their approaches to the task of analysing relations between head office and the site agents, but yet decide that each had something to say that should help to improve relationships between the site agent and head office.

SUMMARY

Writers on organization have looked at the subject from different points of view. Three groups can be distinguished. The oldest is the classical school, which has concentrated on prescribing how the formal organization should be designed and on drawing up principles of good organization which should be generally applicable. Writers in this school stressed the need to clarify responsibilities and authority.

The human relations school, dating from the Hawthorne studies in the 1920s, has studied people's needs and reactions and sought to explain them. It has stressed the need to be aware of these reactions when designing the formal structure. It has shown not only how the formal organization can affect people's behaviour, but also how people may develop their own informal organization. It has helped to explain people's behaviour, and likely reactions to organizational changes, by pointing out how their needs and interests shape their behaviour. It has also encouraged an awareness of the conflicts of interest that exist within organizations.

A more recent way of looking at an organization is as a system. This approach has highlighted the importance of the interactions between different parts of the organization, and between it and its environment. Those who have been more narrowly concerned with information systems have shown how one can look at an organization as a mechanism for processing information for decision-makers.

Each group has made a contribution to the understanding of how organizations work. Each has its limitations. All can be helpful to the manager. One approach may be more useful in tackling a particular problem, though for many problems an understanding of all these different viewpoints is necessary.

An example was given of the ways in which the different viewpoints could be used in looking at a specific problem, and the contributions that each could make to its solution.

NOTES

1. Gareth Morgan, *Images of Organization* (Beverly Hills, Cal., London, New Delhi: Sage 1986).
2. For example, G. H. Fayol, *Industrial and General Management* (London: Pitman, 1948); J. D. Mooney and A. C. Reiley, *The Principles of Organization* (New York: Harper, 1939); L. Urwick, *Notes on the Theory of the Organization* (New York: American Management Association, 1952); E. F. L. Brech, *Organization: The Framework of Management*, 2nd edn (London: Longmans, 1965).
3. F. J. Roethlisberger and William J. Dickson, *Management and the Worker* (Cambridge, Mass.: Harvard University Press, 1939).
4. L. G. Bolman and T. E. Deal, *Modern Approaches to Understanding and Managing Organizations* (San Francisco, 1984; London: Jossey–Bass, 1989) in a very readable textbook with sections on how to apply different theories, split the human relations approach into two: the human resource approach and the political approach. The latter is a more pessimistic view of human nature and hence of the possibility of promoting collaboration between competing interests in an organization.
5. W. F. Whyte, *Human Relations in the Restaurant Industry* (London: McGraw-Hill, 1948).
6. There is a good discussion of the contributions and limitations of contingency theory in Sandra Dawson, *Analysing Organisations*, 2nd edn (London: Macmillan, 1992) pp. 118–35.
7. E. L. Trist, 'The Evolution of Sociotechnical Systems as a Conceptual Framework and as an Action Research Programme', in A. H. van de Ven and

W. F. Joyce (eds), *Perspectives on Organizational Design and Behaviour* (New York: John Wiley, 1981) summarizes these studies.

8. J. I. Cash Jr, F. Warren McFarlan and J. L. McKenney, *Corporate Information Systems Management: The Issues Facing Senior Executives,* 2nd edn (Homewood, Ill.: Irwin, 1988) gives a perspective and advice on coping with so much more information.

Part II
Tasks of Organization

This section has three chapters. All are about the problems of deciding on the formal organization of work. The first looks at the design of individual jobs. It suggests that there are two main decisions to be made: how specialized should the different jobs be; and how far should the duties of each job be defined? Both are related to the more important general question of what kinds of jobs are satisfying to do. The second chapter discusses the different ways in which jobs can be grouped together to form the structure of the organization. It describes the advantages and disadvantages of different forms of grouping and suggests criteria for choosing between them. The third chapter discusses the problems of coordinating related activities. It describes why coordination is so often a problem and what can be done to reduce it.

2 What Kind of Jobs?

Many managers find it easier to think about personalities than about jobs, to think about the way in which Mary does, or fails to do, her work, than to think about the kind of job that Mary is being asked to do. Managers must think about personalities, but they also need to think about jobs and about the demands that these jobs make on people. This means thinking both about the nature of the work that has to be done and about how this work can best be allocated.

The analysis of work is carried out by specialists in work study, in organization and methods, and by personnel staff trained in job analysis. These techniques are described in the appropriate specialist books. The aim of this chapter is to discuss the questions that managers should ask themselves before they make use of such techniques. They must first decide what kind of jobs they want to create and why. They may also want to review whether existing jobs are suited to the organization's current needs and to those of the individual job holders.

There are two questions that ought to be considered by any manager who is deciding about the division of work, or who is thinking about job content:

1. How much specialization should there be?
2. How well-defined should the job be?

These will be the main questions considered in this chapter. Both must be related to the more important question of how to create satisfying jobs.

Before we look at these questions it is worth reminding ourselves how large a part tradition still plays in determining who does what kind of job. This is still true of the division of work between the sexes, though what that tradition is varies considerably from one culture to another. In some countries heavy manual work is thought unsuitable for women; in others no difference is made between the sexes; and in yet others it is the women rather than the men who do it. In the political sphere women have been prime ministers of Great Britain, Norway, France, Iceland, India, Sri Lanka and Israel, but a woman elected as president of the United States of America is, at present, unlikely. In other spheres the division of work between the sexes in the Western world is becoming less clear cut, though the majority of women still do many of the lower paid jobs.

HOW MUCH SPECIALIZATION?

The general trend in modern society has been towards increasing specialization, though recently there have been some changes in the other direction. The distinction is some companies between specialist and generalist is
now less pronounced. However, such broad changes do not tell us what is
the right answer to our question for particular jobs. Sometimes greater specialization is inevitable; sometimes less specialization may seem desirable.
Managers should weigh up the relative advantages and disadvantages of
specialization. They should ask themselves whether the expected benefits,
which may be widely proclaimed, are worth the price. The fact that there is
usually a price to pay may be overlooked.

The contraction of organizations in response to market or governmental
pressures and the need for rapid adaptation are reasons for a recent decline
in specialization. A quite different reason is the recognition that narrowly
specialized manual and clerical jobs may exact a price, that of worker dissatisfaction, which may show itself in poor productivity, industrial unrest,
absenteeism or high labour turnover. Yet another reason is that the skill
content of some jobs is reduced by technical changes.

A distinction should be made between specialization in technical, professional and managerial jobs, and specialization in manual and clerical
ones. Specialization means narrowing the range of work to be done. When
the work is based on knowledge, specialization can create problems,
although the job can still be a challenging and interesting one. Specialization in manual and clerical jobs makes the work more routine.

Specialization of Knowledge Jobs

The expansion of knowledge produces new specialities and leads to the
subdivision of old ones. Large organizations provide both the need and the
economic justification for greater specialization. A growing emphasis on
professionalism leads to the development of new specialists who are formally trained to do a more restricted job than their predecessors.

The trend to greater professionalism has had its impact on the content of
many jobs. This growing professional specialization is exemplified in the
job of chief nurse in a hospital. The occupant of this post was formerly
called matron, and was once in charge of the laundry and of catering as
well as of nursing services. Now the larger hospitals employ outside cater-
ers or have appointed catering officers – the creation of a new specialist job
– while the laundry is the responsibility of a laundry manager or is put out

to a laundry firm. The employment of personnel officers is a further example of professionalizing part of the matron's job.

In business and other organizations new specialist posts are frequently created. Sometimes these are to make use of new technical developments, more often they are a response to a new perceived management need. The new posts may be able to make a sufficient contribution to the company to pay for all the costs of their appointment, though it should not be forgotten that these costs are much more than their salaries and the salaries of their, probably increasing, staff. There is a danger, however, that the appointment of a new type of specialist may not reflect a real need in the organization but merely be a response to fashion. Joan Woodward quoted the example of the materials controller appointed by one company in the area she was studying, followed shortly afterwards by similar appointments by three neighbouring companies.[1] The danger of responding to fashion remains as great today, as any reader of job advertisements can notice.

Greater specialization of knowledge jobs is inevitable, but this does not mean that what is true in general is necessarily advantageous in a particular instance. An example is the argument about making the best use of the time of nurses and teachers. One view is that where there is a shortage of people trained in particular skills, such as nurses or teachers, their time should not be wasted in tasks that could be done by somebody less highly trained. Hence the view that teachers should not have to supervise school meals nor should nurses have to distribute meals or perform many of the other unskilled services for a patient. The narrowing of the range of nurses' duties, however, illustrates the need to consider the possible disadvantages of greater specialization, as well as the advantages. One such disadvantage of the more 'efficient' use of a nurse's time is that she is then seen by the patient only when she gives treatment, which may often be unpleasant. If she also has to perform other duties it allows her to spend more time with the patient and establish a more therapeutic relationship. Here, as with other decisions on whether to introduce greater specialization, managers must ask themselves what is really meant by greater efficiency and by the best use of resources. They can only answer this meaningfully by considering whether the change will further the objectives of the organization. Will patient care, for example, be improved if the nurse is relieved of non-nursing duties? The answer, as in so many organizational questions, will probably have to be found by weighing the advantages and disadvantages of different courses of action; the advantage of using scarce nursing resources on the most skilled jobs against the disadvantage described above. Like many other organizational changes, the disadvantages of the change begin to be more evident after a time and there may be at least a partial change back. This is true in some hospitals which have moved back to the earlier view that there are benefits in nurses being involved in a wide range of tasks for their patients, even if some of them can be carried out by other, less highly trained, staff.

One price of specialization is sufficiently widely recognized to have become an aphorism: 'A specialist is someone who knows more and more about less and less.' As knowledge of a particular subject expands, this must be so; breadth of understanding must, at least to some extent, be sacrificed to more specialized knowledge. In medicine this poses problems in diagnosis; top management in large companies used to worry more about how to teach their specialist junior and middle managers to think more broadly about the business as a whole so that they in turn would be well prepared to take over as senior managers themselves. Now decentralization into smaller and more autonomous units and more movement across functions have reduced the dangers of narrow specialist career paths.

Job Enlargement and Job Enrichment

Many manual, and some clerical, jobs involve little or no skill; the tasks that have to be done have been so subdivided that little training is required, this being the end result of a long process of making these jobs more routine. However, the efficiency of maximum task specialization for manual and clerical work has been questioned by a number of writers and research workers, as well as by the management of a few companies.

The attack on the over-specialization of manual and clerical work has a long history dating from the 1950s. It was followed by studies of how to to design more satisfying jobs, which continue to the present day.[2] Writers such as Argyris, Friedmann, Hackman and Oldham argued that purely repetitive work is not a humane use of human beings, who will have many abilities that will not be utilized in such jobs. Argyris suggested that the requirements of many jobs are the complete opposite of what we expect from a mature adult, and are therefore psychologically unhealthy. He urged the need to try to change organizations so as to provide a more satisfying working environment for people, and to reduce the unproductive activities which result from organizations that are ill suited to people's needs. Friedmann discussed the nature of work, and argued for the merits of job enlargement, describing the experience of some companies who have experimented with it.

McGregor attacked the assumptions about human motivation that lie behind much work organization. He distinguished two opposing management theories about what makes people work and hence what is the best way to organize work – Theory X, the traditional view, and Theory Y.[3] Those who believe in Theory X – that most people are lazy, dislike work and responsibility and will avoid them if they can – will think that the simpler and the more easily controlled the job is, the better. Managements who believe in Theory Y think that most people prefer to work, and want to work better at a job that provides some challenge.

A more recent contrast between opposing views of people at work was given in the *Report of the Tripartite Steering Group on Job Satisfaction*, which said:

> Two contrasting alternative views of people at work are becoming more apparent. One appears to see people as objects. Phrases such as 'head count' are used; collective words like 'workforce', 'management' are adopted; individuality is deliberately lost. The other sees people as agents to get things done by use of initiative, creativity and skill. The behaviour each of these contrasting views creates and the responses such behaviour stimulates have important bearings on the effectiveness of enterprises.[4]

The phrase used by earlier writers was job enlargement, the main emphasis being on an horizontal increase in the scope of jobs by putting together the tasks of several routine jobs. This was later criticized on the ground that adding a number of dreary tasks together does not necessarily make a satisfying job. The term 'job enrichment' is now preferred. It means a vertical change in job content which increases the scope and responsibilities of more junior jobs.

There are now many examples where work has been redesigned for different kinds of jobs so as to motivate people to work well. The lessons are discussed in Hackman and Oldham's book *Work Redesign*.[5] They conclude that people will be motivated to work if they feel that their work is meaningful, that they are responsible for the outcome of the work and that they know the results of their work. Three characteristics of work contribute to its being seen as meaningful:

1. It requires a variety of different activities involving the use of different skills and talents, that is, it provides some challenge.
2. It requires completion of a 'whole', that is, doing a job from start to finish with a visible outcome.
3. The job affects other people's welfare.

People's feeling of responsibility for the outcome of the work is increased by the amount of autonomy that they have in scheduling the work and in determining the procedures to be used in doing it. In routine jobs, control over the speed and rhythm of work gives workers freedom to vary their pace. The greater the autonomy for the jobholder, the more individuals will see the outcome of the work as depending upon their efforts. Motivation also depends upon knowing the results of one's work; that is, having clear and direct information about the effectiveness of one's performance.

Hackman and Oldham argue that a job must be high in at least one of the three characteristics – meaningfulness, responsibility and feedback – if the job is to be motivating, and they go on to describe how to rate jobs as to their capacity to motivate those who hold them. The main lesson for the manager is that he or she should try to design jobs that encourage people to be productive by motivating them to work well. That having been said, however, allowance must be made for individual differences in what people want from work and in their capabilities.

Hackman and Oldham provide guidelines for planning work redesign. Obviously the first step is to decide whether there is a need for work redesign and, next, whether it is feasible. Then there is an important choice; whether to enrich individual jobs or to create self-managing work teams. Their advice is that if both are feasible one should opt for the group design 'only if it is substantially more attractive than the best possible individual design'.[6] The reason for their advice is that it is much harder to develop a group design than to change individual jobs, partly because the former requires more changes in organizational practices and managerial styles than does the latter.

Enthusiasm for job redesign should be tempered by recognizing that there are often trade-offs to be made between advantages and disadvantages of the change. The results may not be wholly positive from management's point of view. Job enrichment may lead to more errors, to demands for higher pay and to more stress.

Job enrichment is only one way of looking at job design. It seeks to improve motivation to do the work well or to reduce labour turnover and absenteeim. It was a reaction to the earlier aim of trying to improve efficiency by making jobs as routine and mechanized as possible. Two other approaches to job design are very important in some jobs. One is ergonomics, which aims to mimimize the physical costs and risks of a job – new jobs can produce new hazards like those that come from working too long at a computer. The other and more recent approach aims to reduce the likelihood of errors and accidents, for example, in nuclear plants. It seeks to ensure that the job design, including the equipment and environment in which it takes place, does not exceed people's mental capabilities and limitations.[7]

HOW WELL DEFINED SHOULD THE JOB BE?

Most, but not all, managers would say that when new jobholders are appointed they should be told what are the job's responsibilities. Some argue that people – by which they mean technical and managerial staff – should create their own jobs. One manager likened the recruitment of a new manager to the act of throwing a single pebble on a pile of pebbles, making the whole pile shift a little.

More usually, however, disagreement arises about how specifically one should spell out job responsibilities. Those who favour doing so in considerable detail argue that it is the only way to avoid ambiguities and to ensure that all the work that needs doing has been analysed and assigned; it is also, they point out, useful as a framework for appraising performance. Those who object to a detailed description of responsibilities say that it makes people take too narrow a view of their job and see it as being bounded by and limited to the specified responsibilities, even though other work may need to be done. They may also object because they think that the rapidity of change makes job descriptions get rapidly out of date and so of little value.

A good argument in support of job description is that they force the compiler to think more clearly about the functions of a job. This is most necessary when an appointment is going to be made. Management may merely say 'We need a good person in the sales department', but unless they think *why* they need a good person and *what* they want done they will not know what kind of man or woman they should be looking for, nor how the job is to fit in with existing jobs. The preparation of a job description can help to ensure that they are asking themselves the right questions.

The more scope there is for initiative in a job – that is, the less the requirements of the job are, or can be, precisely defined – the more choices the jobholder has about what work to do. The United States presidency is an outstanding example of this. The extent to which an individual can choose what work to do in a job usually depends on the kind and level of the job and the climate and type of organization, as well as on the individual's own abilities. In general, the more senior the job the more opportunities there are for the individual to choose what work to do. Managing directors have the greatest scope for doing so as they can decide which aspects of their varied job they think most important or find most congenial. The choice will often be determined by their own functional background; an accountant is likely to see the job of a managing director in a different way from that of a former head of the research department. The scope for individuals to shape a job will also depend on how bureaucratic is the organization for which they work. A very bureaucratic organization will have precise terms of reference for each job and may not allow managers any say in the appointment of their staff – one obvious way in which a manager can determine the character of a department or section.

The smaller the organization, the more the manager may be able to change or even to create the job. In a very large organization there are likely to be more specific posts to be filled, although there may also be new staff jobs that permit their first holders to work out what their role should be. In all organizations there is some choice between a policy of trying to select people for jobs and one of allowing them to make their own jobs. Which choice is made will probably be partly determined by management philosophy and partly by the organization's need for stability or flexibility.

Managers who have to decide how far the responsibilities and tasks of a job should be defined should ask:

- 'Do I believe that people should be allowed wide scope to choose to do the work that suits their abilities?'
- 'Do I believe in telling people what the needs are and then leaving it to them to decide how they should best be met?'
- 'Do I believe that the uncertainties and frictions that such a belief is likely to create between managers are more fruitful than harmful?'

The manager who says 'Yes' to these questions will seek to appoint good people and expect them, at least in part, to create their own jobs. Managers who favour the classical approach to organization, or who are temperamentally in favour of order and clarity, will believe that it is better to describe clearly both what the responsibilities and the duties of each job are and how these are related to other jobs. They will believe in defining the job and then looking for a suitable person to fill it. Yet they should not delude themselves that they can define precisely what should be done and expect a manager to do it. In practice, any responsible job offers scope for individuals to emphasize some aspects of the job and to ignore or minimize others. Studies by the author show how very differently managers in similar jobs can spend their time. They differ in what they do as well as, what is more commonly recognized, in how they do it. In some jobs no one will have the time, the interests or the ability to do all the useful work that could be done. In such jobs it is inappropriate to think of selecting a manager to fit the job; the selection task is to find the person who will choose to concentrate on those aspects of the job that currently most need attention.[8]

Individuals who are looking for a job need to think of what kind of organization will suit their temperament best. Do they feel happier if they know where they are? If their relations with other people are part of a prescribed pattern? Or do they want to be free to exercise as much initiative as possible? It is important that both those who are filling jobs and those who are doing the selection should know which type of job it is and, therefore, what kind of person is suitable for it.

The question of how far the duties of a job should be defined is only one aspect of the wider problem of how formalized should the organization be; that is, how far positions, tasks and procedures should be formally laid down. This, one of the major problems of organization, will be discussed in a later chapter.

SUMMARY

Most managers at times need to think about the content of a particular job. They should ask themselves what kind of job they want to create and why?

One characteristic of jobs is how specialized they are. Increasing knowledge, the development of large organizations and a greater emphasis on professionalism have all led to more specialization of managerial and technical jobs. This is often inevitable, but managers should always ask themselves whether it is desirable in a particular instance. There is a danger of creating new posts that are just a response to a fashion.

There has been a long process of making manual and clerical jobs more specialized by reducing their skill content. The desirability of doing so has been increasingly questioned by some writers, who have argued that many such jobs make unproductive use of human beings and in consequence create undesirable reactions. The price that an organization may have to pay in poorly motivated employees with low productivity, high absenteeism and high staff turnover has led to an interest in various methods of altering jobs in order to make them more motivating. These methods are called job enlargement, job enrichment or, more generally, work redesign. They have now been applied long enough, and to a sufficiently wide variety of jobs, for there to be clear guidelines as to what characteristics of work encourage good motivation: the work should be felt to be meaningful: employees should be able to feel responsible for what they do, and should know the results of their work. An enthusiasm for changing the nature of jobs, to accord with the findings of what makes for a satisfying job, needs to be tempered by recognizing that there can be disadvantages as well as advantages of work redesign. In some jobs the physical and/or mental strains that they impose also need to be considered.

Managers have to decide how far the duties of a job should be defined. The site of the organization, the position in the hierarchy, and the tasks to be done will all affect the amount of flexibility that is possible, as will the organization's relative need for order compared with flexibility. Much can also depend on top management's philosophy; in general, does it believe that a man or woman should be given wide scope to exercise their initiative or should they be selected for a well-defined post?

NOTES

1. Joan Woodward, *Industrial Organization: Theory and Practice* (Oxford: Oxford University Press, 1965) p. 22.
2. Chris Argyris, *Personality and Organization* (New York: Harper, 1957); *Integrating the Individual and the Organization* (New York: John Wiley, 1964); Georges Friedmann, *The Anatomy of Work: The Implications of Specialization* (London: Heinemann, 1961); J. Richard Hackman and Greg R. Oldham, *Work Redesign* (Reading, Mass.: Addison-Wesley, 1980).
3. Douglas McGregor, *The Human Side of Enterprise* (New York: McGraw-Hill, 1960).
4. Work Research Unit, *Report of the Tripartite Steering Group on Job Satisfaction* (London: Her Majesty's Stationery Office, 1982) p. 5.
5. Hackman and Oldham, *Work Redesign*, pp. 77–88.
6. Ibid., p. 224.
7. M. A. Campion and P. W. Thayer, 'Job Design: Approaches, Outcomes, and Trade-offs', *Organizational Dynamics* (Winter 1987)' provide a simple and practical guide to different approaches to job design and to the outcomes that they seek to achieve. They emphasize that trade-offs are likely to be necessary between the costs and benefits of two or more of them.
8. Rosemary Stewart, *Choices for the Manager: A Guide to Managerial Work and Behaviour* (Maidenhead, Berks.: McGraw-Hill; Englewood Cliffs, N. J.: Prentice-Hall, 1982).

3 How to Group Activities

Jobs in organizations cannot exist in isolation. They have to be related to each other. This is called 'grouping' or, an unappealing word, 'departmentalization'. This chapter is about the different ways in which work can be grouped and the criteria that managers should use to help them decide which is the most appropriate for their circumstances.

Sometimes the grouping of jobs causes no problems. In a canteen the waitresses will clearly be grouped together, as will the kitchen staff. Both groups will report to their own supervisor, who will report in turn to the canteen manager. So far there are few or no problems in deciding the right form of grouping. But who should the canteen manager report to? There may be no obvious answer. In companies it is often the personnel manager, but may be the works manager or the head of administrative services. It may not matter what decision is made, as the canteen is a relatively self-contained activity which is unlikely to be much affected by the place of its manager in the organization. Because it is a self-contained activity, it is now often given to an outside contractor to manage. More and more managements have been deciding that activities that are not central to the organization's purpose would be better run by companies for whom they are a core activity.

The problem of finding the best place for the computer department has proved much more complex over the years than the location of the canteen. The decision about the grouping of an activity matters most when the nature of the activity will be affected by it. Unlike the canteen, what the computer department does depends in part on where it is in the organization. When computing facilities were centred on a large central computer the department which managed this facility acquired power. This was an argument against putting the computer under the control of the finance department, as was frequently the case, because doing so could discourage other departments from making adequate use of it. The development of personal computers and individual terminals have made the grouping of the data processing facilities less important. The factory side of the work can, Earl suggests 'be run anywhere, locally, regionally, centrally or even outsourced (contracted out) – and should be decided according to criteria of efficiency and reliability'.[1]

What was the computer department is now often called the IT department (Information Technology (IT): the collection, processing, storage and transmitting of information by electronic means). The growing contribution that the IT department can make to the business makes its location important. Earl argues that since IT can now make a contribution to business strategy it must be well integrated into the business. He says that two organizational choices for locating IT are mistaken. One is to hive IT off as a separate business venture: this no longer fits the demands of the 1990s because it will not be close enough to the business's strategic decisions. The other is to have a totally centralized IT function in a decentralized organization: this will be too remote from the sharp end of the business.[2]

TYPES OF GROUPING

A manager who has to decide where to place an activity in the organization will find it useful to know what types of grouping are available and what are their advantages and disadvantages. A knowledge of the types of grouping becomes still more important when the manager is thinking about building a new organization or reorganizing an existing one. The main types of groupings are described below.

It is helpful for managers to examine their plans for grouping against these different categories, as doing so may give them a better idea of the advantages and disadvantages of what they are proposing. Unfortunately, they may find a conflict between the categories. All they can do is to try to choose the grouping which best seems to suit the present needs of their particular organization. Time may show them that they overrated the advantages of the form of grouping that they chose and that they overlooked or underrated some of the disadvantages.

Products or Services

Different products made by the same company may require their own specialized equipment and their own expertise. Where this is so, grouping by product is often found to be a convenient way of dividing up the company into fairly self-contained parts. Grouping by product is most common in large diversified companies, where it is seen as a way of reducing some of the problems of size by creating semi-autonomous units. The advantages of this type of grouping is that it brings together all those with special knowledge of the product, and makes easier the coordination of activities such as purchasing, production and sales that are associated with it. Grouping by product is also often used within a department, as when the sales or purchasing departments are subdivided into sections for each of the main products.

All the activities associated with a particular service may also be grouped together, as they may be in the transport department (it can be argued that this is also functional grouping, which is described below). Whether to create separate service departments or to provide each establishment or department with its own services is one of the common problems in large organizations. Managers often prefer to have control over the services they use, such as engineering or personnel. Services that need expensive communal equipment, such as canteens or in hospitals, radiology, and, formerly, computers, or that must work to very stringent standards, may need to be grouped together more than services that can be rendered by individuals with their own equipment such as word processors.

Functions

This is a commonly used basis for grouping in all types of organizations.[3] In some, where the heads of the main functional departments report to the chief executive, it is the dominant one. In others it is a subsidiary one, as in a product division where the general manager may be in charge of functional heads.

The typical functions of a manufacturing company are production, marketing and sales, engineering, finance, purchasing and personnel. In some manufacturing companies research and development is essential and so must be a separate function. The relative importance of marketing and sales varies greatly from one type of business to another, as will the size of the department and its relative importance in the hierarchy. Only a careful analysis of the activities of the organization will show which are sufficiently important to be organized as separate functions.

Specialization is the main advantage of grouping by function. It brings together the specialized knowledge needed for that particular activity, and also helps to ensure that adequate attention is given to it. The latter is the reason for the creation of new functional departments such as public relations. Specialization, as we saw in the last chapter, also has its disadvantages, however. Functional grouping can make people narrow-minded, so that they concentrate on their own speciality and know and care little about the other activities in their organization, and there is always the danger that people will put the interests of their own function above that of the organization as a whole. The larger the organization the greater the danger that functional grouping will lead to the growth of specialized and myopic departments that are hard to coordinate. Hence the creation of separate product groups in many large manufacturing companies, and the use of functional grouping as a subsidiary rather than as the main form of departmentalization.

'Function' is a very general label and does not describe what particular activities will be included, nor the level at which different activities are grouped. Marketing and sales, for example, may have two heads reporting to the managing director, or there may be only one marketing director, the split between marketing and sales being made lower down. Human resources is another illustration of an activity that can either have only one functional head, with individual functional departments or sections below him, or be subdivided at top management level; training and development, for example, may be made a separate top-level appointment. (Human resource management is the title which, following American practice, is increasingly replacing 'personnel'.) Where the division is made will depend upon the importance that is attached to the different activities and, often, too, to the political abilities of individuals in getting their activity promoted in the hierarchy.

Customers

Grouping by customers means separate groups for different types of customer. This form of organization is most appropriate in sales departments that sell to very different markets, such as domestic and industrial consumers or home and export sales; separate grouping enables their particular requirements to be catered for more knowledgeably. The same applies to the distinction made in hospitals between medical and surgical wards, and the creation of separate children's wards.

Canteens lend themselves to a variety of different types of customer grouping:

- one canteen for everyone;
- several canteens, open to all, but providing different standards at different prices – grouping by service;
- grouping by different types of customers, either by type of work – clean or dirty – by level in the hierarchy, or, as in some hospitals, by function;
- there may also, in a large spread-out works, be canteens in different locations – this is grouping by place, which is discussed below.

The decision that is made about the canteen will, as in most grouping decisions, have to weigh a number of considerations. Is it desirable to provide one category of employees with a higher standard of food and service than another category, or to provide lower-paid employees with a cheaper meal than higher-paid staff? Should one make it easier for one group of employees to talk together at mealtimes, even though this reduces the opportunity for them to have informal contacts with other groups? And what are the preferences of the different groups themselves? These may vary from one type of organization to another and from one part of the country to another: workers may prefer to eat separately from their bosses; managers may think a high-grade manager's dining room an essential promotion perk. When customer grouping is bedevilled by such status feelings it is very hard to decide what is the best organization! Even if the decision is increasingly to have the same canteen for everyone, management may find that, in practice, employees segregate themselves by coming in at different times or by sitting at different tables.

Place

This is an important basis for grouping where services to customers or clients can be economically provided within a limited area, or where – as for a hospital, school or post office – it is most convenient for the customer if the service is nearby. Customer convenience, though, may be overridden by other considerations such as economy, as it has been in the closing of many of the smaller post offices.

It may be easy to decide that grouping by place is necessary for some consumer goods and services. The more difficult problem is to decide what is the right size for each grouping. This problem arises in an acute form in discussions on regionalization and the right pattern for local government and for the health service.

Time

Organizations that employ workers on shifts, whether in industry, hospitals or elsewhere, will have separate groups for different shifts. Should each shift do the same kind of work? The answer may be clearly 'Yes', as in continuous shift working, though more maintenance may be done on one shift than another. Should different shifts do different tasks? There may be no choice: night nursing is bound to be different from day nursing; in a computer department that is on three shifts, longer and more straightforward runs will be done at night as they will generate fewer queries. In some forms of organization there may be more choice as to what each shift should do. Trist and Bamforth, in a classic study, found that one of the troubles with the conventional longwall method of coal-mining was that each shift was responsible for a different phase of coal-getting, and that this contributed to the friction that existed between the shifts. Relations were much better when groups of workers, with members in each shift, were made responsible for a complete work cycle.[4]

Examples of Types of Grouping

Organization charts can show which type or types of grouping has been adopted. Figure 3.1 shows grouping by product in a diversified company, Figure 3.2 grouping by function, while Figure 3.3 illustrates how a number of different types of grouping – product, function and area (place) – may be used in the same organization. In this last illustration, product grouping is the primary one.

CRITERIA FOR GROUPING

Most organizations contain examples of several of the above types of grouping. How can a manager decide which type or combination of types is best? There are no definite answers, but among the large number of different criteria that have been suggested, the ones described below seem the most useful.

The relative importance of these different criteria will depend upon one's aims. If one is clear about the purpose of an activity it is easier to decide how much weight to give to the different criteria. A change in purpose may lead to a change in their relative importance. The purpose of mental hospitals, for example, has been changing, from that of predominantly custodial institutions, when the organization of separate and geographically remote units was thought appropriate, to therapeutic, often short-stay establishments which can be included in a general hospital and which are used to support the shift from institutional to community-based care.

Good coordination

This is a major problem in most organizations, so the type of grouping that will minimize the problem must have a lot to be said for it. The larger the organization the more weight must be given to this criterion. This is why the specialist advantages of functional grouping may be outweighed in large organizations by the disadvantages of poor coordination.

Two other criteria which are sometimes given can be put under the general heading of coordination. One is the criterion of use, which suggests

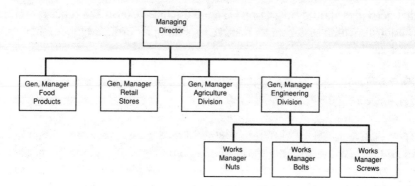

Figure 3.1 *Grouping by Product*

Figure 3.2 *Grouping by Function*

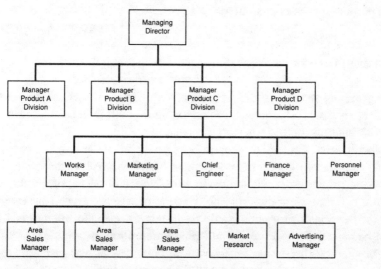

Figure 3.3 *Multi-type Groupings*

that activities should be grouped around the main users. The other criterion is control, which suggests that activities should be grouped where they can most easily be controlled.

Economy

The relative costs of different forms of grouping is another factor that should be considered. Other criteria may outweigh the arguments for economy, but at least the cost of alternative forms of grouping should, as far as possible, be assessed. For example, one form of grouping may need more equipment than another, more staff, or use more expensive office space. Some organizations, both business and Civil Service, have moved part of their staff out of London after deciding that some activities were sufficiently self-contained that they could be physically separated from the expensive London offices.

Use of Specialist Knowledge

The manager should decide how important specialist knowledge is, and *which* kind of specialist knowledge is most useful. Where specialist knowledge is in short supply, this criterion will have extra weight. Grouping by product brings together those with specialist knowledge of the product. Grouping by type of customer puts the emphasis on specialist knowledge of a particular type of customer.

Clarity of Division of Work

The grouping should, as far as possible, avoid ambiguity about the work to be done, and who should do it. Such ambiguity will increase the problems of coordination, so this criterion is related to the first.

Uncertainty as to which department or which section is responsible for work can lead to conflict. This is most likely to arise at the boundaries between groupings; hence the desirability, where possible, of dividing the groups by some clear-cut criterion. Uncertainty cannot always be avoided, but the method of grouping should try to minimize it. However, there may also be dangers in too precise and rigid a definition of who does what, as we saw in the discussion on job descriptions; it can, for instance, cause delay if the person on the spot says 'It is not my job to do so and so.'

Minimizing Conflict

Disharmonies and inefficiencies can arise from a grouping that has been made purely from technical considerations, without regard to the effects that it has on the workers involved. Research by members of the Tavistock Institute of Human Relations showed this; they used the phrase 'socio-technical systems' to describe the fact 'that any production system requires both a technological organization – equipment and process layout – and a work organization relating to each other those who carry out the necessary tasks'.[5] Sometimes the technical requirements may not allow alternative work groupings, but where they do the manager should try and take into account the likely effects of different types of grouping on relationships, both those between the workers and those between them and their supervisors.

The criterion of avoiding conflict should also be applied to the grouping of new activities. Those responsible for the organizational decision should ask themselves 'What benefits does control of this activity offer?' This question should be asked of the human resource management and planning departments, both of which may in time affect the relative power and status of other departments.

Appreciation of Local Conditions

The need to recognize local conditions is one of the reasons for grouping by place. It is an important consideration in some sales and service organizations.

MATRIX ORGANIZATION

All forms of grouping have their disadvantages. Each of those described so far focus on one basis for grouping. A matrix organization combines two. It developed in the 1960s in some companies experiencing rapid complex change. For example, in the American aerospace industry it developed, according to Kingdon,[6] because a project management system was a requirement for government contracts, and this was superimposed horizontally upon the functional specialist departments. Individual engineers could then be working both in a specialist department, reporting to a boss there, and in a project team composed of members from different departments and under the charge of a project manager. They would thus have two bosses. This was called a matrix organization because it could be portrayed as a grid with functional departments along the top and projects, products or business areas along the side – last two because matrix organization is not only used for project teams.

Kingdon describes the matrix organization as a compromise, a way of reconciling two sets of needs:

> The customer's need to deal with one person who is responsible for the project. The organization's need for continuity so that it can handle future projects because it retains the strong functional departments, whose members can be reallocated to new inter-departmental projects which may require different expertise.

It is a compromise, between the efficiency that can come from specialist departments with formalized procedures and the flexibility that is needed to handle complex changing situations.

Kenneth Knight, who has been the leading British exponent of matrix organization, argues the need for managers to have concepts for thinking about the appropriate organization structure. He suggests that the concept of matrix can be helpful:

> Where an organization is under pressure to develop new products or institute new services involving the collaboration of different functions and specialists, organizational options have to be considered. One of the broad options available is a matrix structure. Within this there are, of course, various sub-options which will result in differently defined individual roles. But unless the matrix concept is available a whole area of possibility may be overlooked. The idea of crossing lines of authority or influence may simply lack the legitimacy that would allow it to be considered seriously.[7]

All organizational forms have problems. The complexity of matrix structures make them particularly susceptible to problems, so much so that managers should be very wary of considering matrix organization as a structural solution to the problems of managing complex interdepartmental relations. If they think they must do so then they must help managers to develop the flexible perspectives to cope with being pulled in different directions and to be good at negotiating the trade-offs. Bartlett and Ghoshal, writing in the *Harvard Business Review* in 1990, warn about the dangers of thinking of a matrix organization as a structural answer to complex problems rather than thinking primarily about the need to change managers' attitudes and relationships.[8]

DIVISIONALIZATION

Divisionalization is a form of decentralization which consists of dividing a company or a public service organization into a number of operating divisions. Each division is self-contained and autonomous in managing its day-to-day operations. Strategic planning and overall financial control are run by a head office. This form of decentralization has been popular with large companies since the 1960s.

A survey of 144 large UK firms in the mid-1980s found that very few were still organized functionally. Most were divisionalized although some had a holding company with a number of subsidiary companies. No evidence was found to support the claim that companies divided into divisions would be more profitable than those which were not. The researchers suggest that one reason may be that some divisions were themselves groups of companies and needed further decentralization.[9]

The Thatcher government's 'Next Steps', introduced from the late 1980s, was a form of divisionalization of the Civil Service. It consisted of changing operational parts into agencies with their own chief executive and greater freedom to manage themselves within overall control from Whitehall. It was aimed, like divisionalization in companies, at improving accountability and providing a greater stimulus for cost-effective performance.

In the late 1980s and early 1990s the idea behind divisionalization was sometimes taken further by moving from semi-autonomous units to much more, or even completely, independent ones. This was done by splitting off some businesses into separate companies. The reasons for doing so were financial rather than organizational. They made the original company less vulnerable to takeover or, as in the ICI split, made it easier to raise capital for the more profitable businesses.

SPAN OF CONTROL (HOW MANY TO A BOSS?)

In grouping jobs together, a different type of problem from those described so far is that of 'How many jobs should be put under one supervisor or manager?' This is the 'span of control'. As Urwick put it, 'No person should supervise more than five, or at most six direct subordinates whose work interlocks'.[10] Few people nowadays would accept this as it stands, but all would probably think that there are limits to the number of people who can be effectively supervised by one person. What these limits are in any particular situation will depend both upon its characteristics and upon management aims. The amount of control that needs to be exercised and how that can be done are important guides to the span of control. Where the control must be close and has to be exercised personally, then the span of control must be small. Where the control is exercised by company systems, these may replace the need for close supervision by the immediate superior. This is one of the explanations for the wide span of control of the regional manager in charge of a large number of chain store managers.

There are numerous factors to be considered in the situation itself. One of the most important is the experience and knowledge of the people being supervised, and hence the extent to which they may need supervision. Another is the difficulty of the work being done. The more routine the jobs, the greater usually can be the number of people supervised; thus at the bottom of the hierarchy, whether on the shopfloor or in the office, one is likely to find larger spans of control than higher up. Urwick's principle showed another factor that is important – the extent to which the subordinates' work interlocks. The area manager in charge of managers of stores in different towns will only be dealing with their work individually, whereas the manager of a group of people who are in frequent contact with each other will also have to deal with their relations with each other, and any manager will know what problems this can bring!

The phrase 'span of control' itself has an old-fashioned sound. It was of much concern to the classical writers, but in a society which emphasizes leadership and commitment rather than control by superiors it is less important. Yet changes in the span of control are a by-product of, even if not a reason for, a change in the number of levels in the organization. The narrower the span of control the more levels there will be; the organization chart will then look like a steep pyramid, as in Figure 3.4. An organization with wide spans of control will have a much flatter pyramid, with fewer levels, as in Figure 3.5; it will also provide jobs with more scope than in an organization with a narrow span of control and with many tiers. Communication upwards and downwards are likely to be more difficult where there are many levels. This is a disadvantage that should be remembered when opting for a narrow span of control. It will also take a long time for a manager to climb many rungs in the promotion ladder. However, a flat organization has the disadvantage that there are less opportunities for promotion, since there are fewer tiers in the hierarchy. The great pressure on organizations to be cost effective has led to leaner, flatter organizations. The reduced opportunities for promotion are partly, at least, offset by the greater responsibility for middle managers in a flatter organization.

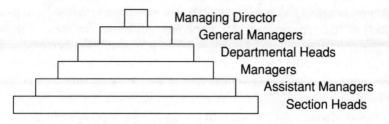

Figure 3.4 *Organization with Narrow Span of Control*

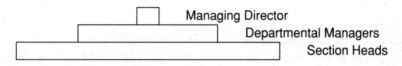

Figure 3.5 *Organization with Wide Span of Control*

SUMMARY

Most managers will, at some time in their careers, have to decide how to group work; that is, how best to combine the different activities for which they are responsible. Before they decide, they should be clear what are the alternatives. The different forms of grouping are by product or service functions (sometimes called 'process'), by customers, by place and by time. Most organizations include a number of different types of grouping, with one as the primary division and the others as subsidiary.

What is the most suitable form of grouping for the situation must be determined by weighing up the merits and drawbacks of the possible options. There are a number of criteria that can be used for doing so. It will be desirable to try to minimize problems of coordination, but doing so may conflict with the need to take advantage of specialization; in general, the larger the organization the more important does it become to try to facilitate coordination. The relative economics of different forms of grouping should obviously be considered. The grouping should, as far as possible, avoid ambiguity about the work to be done, and about who should do it, though there can also be dangers in being too precise. Some forms of grouping are much more likely than others to generate conflict between individuals and groups, so the avoidance of conflict is another criterion. In some organizations an adequate understanding of local conditions will also be valuable. The relative importance of these different criteria will depend upon the aims of the organization. The changing role played by a particular function will affect decisions about grouping. This was illustrated by the IT department.

Matrix, a form of grouping developed in American aerospace companies in the 1960s, has been adopted in some complex organizations. It combines two forms of grouping, such as a functional department and a project team, so that an individual reports to two bosses. Managers need to be wary of adopting this type of grouping because of the problems that such complex relationships create.

Divisionalization is now popular in most large organizations because it creates more manageable and accountable units. Each division may group its activities in a number of different ways. The main alternative to divisionalization is a functional organization. The creation of more autonomous accountable units, one of the characteristics of divisionalization, has been extended to public-service orientated organizations.

The span of control (that is, number of immediate subordinates reporting to a manager) is another decision to be made when grouping activities. There are limits to the number of people one manager can effectively supervise. What these limits are depend on a variety of factors, including the nature of the work, the extent to which the subordinates' work is interrelated, and how much training and experience they have had and how far control is exercised by peer pressure. The latter is most likely in an organization where employees have a high commitment to its success. Management policy must also affect the span of control. Does management favour tight control, or does it want to stimulate initiative? The former is an argument for a small span, the latter for a large one.

NOTES

1. M. J. Earl, 'Putting IT in its Place: a Polemic for the Nineties', *Journal of Information Technology*, vol. 7 (1992) pp. 105–6.
2. Ibid., pp. 100–8.
3. The classical writers called this 'grouping by process'. It was used in reference to public organizations. Applied to manufacturing industry, it can cause confusion, as grouping by process can refer to the different stages in manufacturing. Hence the term 'functions' is preferable for this type of grouping.
4. E. L. Trist and K. W. Bamforth, 'Some Social and Psychological Consequences of the Longwall Method of Coal Getting', *Human Relations*, vol. 4, no. 1 (1951) pp. 3–38.
5. A. K. Rice, *Productivity and Social Organization: The Ahmedabad Experiment* (London: Tavistock, 1958) p. 4
6. D. R. Kingdon, *Matrix Organization* (London: Tavistock, 1973).
7. Kenneth Knight (ed.), *Matrix Management* (Aldershot, Hants.: Gower, 1977) p. 9

8.   Christopher A. Barlett and Sumantra Ghoshal, 'Matrix Management: Not a Structure, a Frame of Mind', *Harvard Business Review*, July–Aug. 1990, pp. 138–45.

9.   C. W. L. and J. F. Pickering, 'Divisionalization, Decentralization and Performance of Large United Kingdom Companies', *Journal of Management Studies*, January 1986, pp. 26–50.

10. L. Urwick, *The Elements of Administration*, 2nd edn (London: Pitman, 1947) pp. 52–3.

4 Coordination: Problems and Remedies

In the previous chapter we saw that facilitating coordination is an important criterion in grouping. The problem of achieving good coordination is such a difficult one that this chapter is devoted to it.

We are all familiar with stories about how one part of an organization failed to coordinate with another, like the one about the government department that sold surplus goods to a merchant who then made a large profit selling them to another government department. Such stories are told for laughs. To the layman they are ludicrous follies, but the manager, whether in private or public organizations, knows how hard it can be to keep departments adequately informed of each other's activities and needs.

When people work on related activities, these activities must be coordinated so that they contribute most efficiently to the common purpose. To do this is one of the most important and difficult problems of organization. This chapter will look at why there are coordination problems, and will discuss the different methods that can be used to tackle them.

In an ideal organization, coordination would be a task but not a problem. All members would will the good of the organization: that is, they would agree on what was their common purpose and would work together to achieve it; they would be more interested in pursuing the objectives of the organization than in their own individual or departmental interests; they would actively and intelligently seek to ensure that what they did contributed to the efficiency of the whole; they would also be perfectly informed about the effects of their activities on other departments. Such a description, as we all know, does not correspond to any actual organization. Hence, where there is a need for coordination, there is always a problem in trying to achieve it.

The description of what would happen in an ideal organization provides a guide to what can be done to reduce problems of coordination. Members of the organization should know and agree on their common objectives. This statement may be idealistic, but at least it points to the value of defining organizational goals and of trying to ensure that these are widely known and understood. It also means that managers should be encouraged to think in terms of the good of the organization rather than purely that of their own department or division. In the ideal organization we said that members would be perfectly informed of the effects of their activities on other departments. Again, this is difficult to achieve, but much can be done to make it easier.

WHY PROBLEMS ARISE

Coordination problems can arise because people do not know what they should be doing in order to relate their activities to those of other parts of the organization; the problems arise from failures in communication. Similarly, such problems can be created by poor planning, bad work allocation and by poor grouping of activities. More difficult to deal with are the problems that stem from conflict of interest, between individuals, between groups or departments, and between the organization as a whole and its constituent parts. Committees of inquiry into the workings of public bodies suggest that inertia – an unwillingness to take responsibility – may be the most difficult problem of all.

Poor Planning

The more complicated the dovetailing of activities, and the more costly the failure to do so, the more important it becomes to plan properly. Poor planning may be the only explanation of failure of coordination or it may be a contributory one. Poor planning is easier to correct than some of the other causes of poor coordination. There are a number of techniques that aid planning. More important than a knowledge of these techniques is the ability to recognize when planning is essential and what needs to be planned and coordinated.

The planning of new projects will need to consider not only the content of the information that different departments will want in order to keep their activities in step, but also when the information will be required. What, for instance, does the marketing department need to know about a new product and when does it need to know it if it is to plan the marketing effectively? Public relations officers are much concerned with ensuring that reporters get the right information – from the organization's viewpoint – and get it at the right time. The press release is a simple device for trying to coordinate the release of news.

Organization vs Local Interests

A conflict of interests exists if, for example, a subsidiary company's profits are maximized when the subsidiary pursues one course of action but the profit of the company as a whole is greater when the subsidiary pursues an alternative strategy. Such a conflict is increased if the subsidiary is treated as a profit centre and the efficiency of its top management is assessed by the local profits, which may even be the basis for bonus payments. Group services, such as transport, which have to be paid for by those who use them, often result in such a clash of interests; it may be cheaper for the subsidiary company or division to buy the services externally, but if allowance is made for the contribution to overheads it may be more economical for the company as a whole if group services are used.

The extent to which the activities of the different parts of a large organization need to be coordinated will depend upon company policy. At one extreme of centralization, the directors may seek to ensure common policies throughout the organization for all aspects of the business. At the other, the directors of the parent company may only act as banker, set profitability criteria and make the top appointment(s), otherwise leaving each subsidiary or division free to manage in its own way. These are the two extremes. Most large companies will lie between the two, though now more towards the decentralized end. The burden of coordination will therefore be less and will exist mainly within each division rather than at the centre.

The need for coordination, and possibly for a more centralized policy, can arise when the action of one subsidiary or division affects another; for example, when the wages and conditions offered by one part of the company are used as an argument by the unions for demanding similar conditions elsewhere. Where this happens, local management must ask themselves what the repercussions of their actions will be elsewhere in the organization. There may be a conflict of interests for them, at least in the short term: for example between an agreement that they wish to conclude with the unions and the knowledge of what would be best for the organization as a whole. The danger that local management may put their own interests before that of the group as a whole may lead top management to adopt a more centralized industrial relations policy.

The need for coordination may only gradually become recognized, a major current example being provided by information technology (defined on p. 29). In many organizations a number of departments have made their own separate time-consuming investigations about what to buy from the multiplicity of hardware kits and software available. The problem may be partly a conflict between local and organizational interests, often over the length of time that it takes to develop an organizational policy towards information technology, especially when a department may want to go ahead quickly. There may also be a conflict of opinion between local and central specialists. In this area, more and more organizations are attempting to define those decisions needing central coordination and those which can be left to local departments. This is similar to what has happened in other areas of purchasing, but it is rendered more complex because of the very rapid changes in equipment and software and because of the need to develop a strategy for the use of information technology.

Conflicts between Departments

The conflict of interests between sales and production is an ever-present problem in many manufacturing companies. It will, of course, be much reduced if the sales and works managers are genuinely more interested in the company's good than in that of their own departments; then the conflict of interests will be diminished, although there may still be a wide difference in viewpoint, stemming from the special needs and problems of their separate departments. Production will want a steady and predictable rate of production so that they can plan to use their resources of people and machinery as efficiently as possible. They will also prefer to produce only a few varieties of products so as to permit longer runs. The sales department, on the other hand, wants to attract and please customers by providing the variations that they ask for and by supplying goods whenever they are requested. They may make promises to customers about deliveries without consulting the works to see if they can be kept.

Nor is this failure likely to be purely a question of insufficient information about the works' position. Sales may argue – as one can hear them doing in management meetings in very different types of companies – 'If we ask production they will say "No," but if we don't they will manage somehow.' The reverse happens too. Sales complain that they were not consulted about the quantities that they could sell before the works produced them. Production may retort, 'If we produce the stuff they will have to sell it. We have found from experience that they can sell more under pressure than they will admit to in advance.' Both sides may have discovered that they can successfully put pressure on the other in that way. This discovery, and consequent tactics, can become self-defeating if the other department starts to protect itself by saying that it can do less than it anticipates.

The conflict of interests that often arises between production and sales is one illustration of the coordination problems that can result from such differences. The example was chosen as it is one of the commonest and best known, but there are many others. In hospitals there are frequent complaints by nursing and administrative staff of consultants' failure to coordinate their activities with those of other people. Here the problem is that individual consultants may act without thinking of the organizational repercussions of what they do.

Organizational changes may help to reduce conflicts of interest. This was a reason for abolishing the separate Parliamentary under-secretaries for each of the armed services which had, in the past, helped to support the lobbying by each service for the best equipment.

Competition for Services

The typing pool, in itself a fairly simple work unit, can illustrate many of the conflicts of interest that arise when people are competing for scarce resources. A well-run typing pool should try and ensure as even a flow of work as possible so that the typists are not hopelessly over-burdened at one period, with consequent long delays for the customers, nor have too little to do at other times. There is also a need to try to assess priorities at times of pressure so that the most urgent work gets typed first.

Users of typing pools are likely to make these tasks difficult. Many of them think that their work must have priority; few have the foresight to warn the typing pool that they have a large job coming up. The problems for the typing pool are likely to be complicated by the fact that those asking for services may have different pulling power. Differences due to official status can easily be accommodated; it is usually the most senior people who get their work done first. However, there may also be unofficial differences in pulling power, due to friendship or even fear. One manager may get preference because she is so nice or because she is an old buddy; another may get preference because, if she does not, she makes herself unpleasant (though this form of pressure may produce the opposite effect).

The usual way of trying to maximize coordination is to make the typing-pool supervisor responsible for dealing with all requests for typing and for allocation of work. This ensures that one person is responsible for coordination. The supervisor is able to assess the overall load on the unit and is also in a better position than the individual typist to resist pressures.

Failures in Communication

Bad communications are often blamed for various failures. This is thought to be an explanation, whereas it is at best a possible diagnosis, with the causes still to be discovered. The cause may be poor organization of who needs to know what and when. It may be due to poor management attitudes – a good communication system is no substitute for a willingness to cooperate with other managers; hence the need to be aware of sources of conflicts of interest and of the reasons for differences in viewpoint. This is not to underrate the importance of a good communication system in order to ensure that what needs to be communicated is received and understood, but that is of no use if the recipients are not willing to act on the information.

A problem that exists in many organizations, but that is most acute in political life, is to ensure that information is consistent. Ministers must give consistent information, particularly on a subject of public interest, otherwise they will be pursued by their political opponents and the press. This requires an understanding of the potential political sensitivity of an issue so that care can be taken to ensure coordination between different spokesmen.

REDUCING THE PROBLEM

Good organization can help to reduce both the need for, and the problems of, coordination, but the methods that are appropriate in one organization may not be suitable in another where conditions are different. Organizations undergoing a rapid rate of change will tend to have more coordination problems than those that are experiencing little change. Those in a relatively stable environment should have learnt where coordination is necessary and what should be done to achieve it, while those with a rapid rate of change will have to give more attention to promoting it and to trying to foresee the new coordination needs that will arise. Coordination must be an on-going activity if it is to keep up with changing conditions. In today's rapidly changing world new needs for coordination will arise frequently. Therefore, the problem of coordination is never more than temporarily solved. New solutions will always be needed for new problems. However, an alertness to the likelihood of coordination problems can in itself help to reduce them.

Chain of Command

Utilizing a chain of command is one method of coordinating the activities of different individuals and groups. Each manager in charge of subordinates working on related activities must try and ensure that their work is coordinated. It will be a major responsibility in the more hierarchical organizations, but in the more organic ones, particularly where there are many experts, lateral coordination is likely to be a more effective method.

The value of a hierarchy in facilitating coordination has been shown in studies of both laboratory and normal organizations. Blau and Scott, reviewing laboratory studies of the effects on performance of the organization of small groups, concluded that 'hierarchical organization serves important functions of achieving coordination and that it does so specifically by restricting the free flow of communication'.[1] If the groups are hierarchically organized – that is, if they have a leader – he or she assumes the dominant role of coordinator.

Kaufman, in his classic study of how the US Forest Service worked, concluded that 'Hierarchy . . . is certainly one of the ways the Forest Service has avoided the splintering effects of other characteristics of a large and complex agency'.[2] After pointing out that the ranger (the manager in charge of a forest district) issues all instructions to his subordinates and that all superiors must go through him, Kaufman described the advantages of the chain of command as follows:

> The existence, at each level, of a single, determinate individual formally empowered to issue decisions with respect to all functions – decisions not subject to further appeal at the same level – means that the competing claims of the several functional specialities will often be judged in terms of more general criteria of decision. It also relieves higher headquarters of torrents of detail from below that would otherwise impede concentration of the full-time task of maintaining integration. At the same time, it safeguards field units against incessant intervention by functional specialists from above, uncoordinated intervention that could result in hopeless confusion in the field. And it cuts down the problems of communication by establishing, close to the field, 'switchboards' in which general directives are adapted to the specific conditions of limited areas, and in which inconsistencies are often discovered and eliminated before instructions take effect upon field personnel.[3]

The advantages of a clear chain of command, where it exists, can be contrasted with the problems of lack of coordinated effort shown by many public inquiries. Many of these arise from the problems of coordinating the work of different public bodies. This is a much more difficult task than coordination in a strongly hierarchical organization. How difficult is being shown in the attempts to provide 'seamless care' in the community by coordination between the health services, local authorities and voluntary bodies.

Good Grouping

Coordination problems are made harder in organizations with strong functional divisions. They are exacerbated where, as in local government and the health services, there are strong professional hierarchies and careers are structured within them. When deciding on the organizational groupings in schools, universities, local government, the health services and so on, the relative merits of strong specialisms should be weighed carefully against the coordination problems that may result.

The way in which activities are grouped can help to reduce the amount of coordination that is necessary and can make it easier to achieve. Unfortunately, there are, as we saw in the previous chapter, other criteria for grouping which may be considered more important than that of easing problems of coordination. Where this is so it is even more important to think about coordination needs. Managers should ask themselves 'Where are there likely to be coordination problems?' and 'What can we do to reduce them?' More simply, they can ask 'Who will need to talk to whom?' and 'What are we doing to make it easy for them to do so?' They can also ask 'What can we do to make it easier for them to understand each other when they do talk?' Common experience is one answer to the last question, ranging from promotions across departments to sports and dramatic activities.

Formal Meetings

The word 'committee' may be used narrowly for a pre-arranged meeting with an agenda and minutes, or more broadly. Most definitions include the idea that committees are groups that are formed to accomplish specific objectives.

Grumbling about the time spent in committees and other formal meetings is a favourite managerial pastime in some organizations, although this is more likely to be a reflection of the way the committees work, or rather fail to work, than a necessary condemnation of committees as such. Many may feel sympathy at times, both with the person who said 'In a committee minutes are taken but hours are wasted' and with the view that 'The ideal committee consists of three people, with two people absent'. Yet many would admit, perhaps with regret, that committees are often a necessary means of coordination.

The amount of time spent in meetings obviously varies considerably, even in companies of the same size. It is likely to be greatest in large organizations; half or more of top managers' time in some large organizations is spent in formal meetings. Luthans comments:

> Most committees seem to serve as a focal point for the exchange of different viewpoints and information. There is considerable evidence that the use of committees is directly related to the size of the organization.[4]

Committees, though they are a useful and, sometimes, indispensable means of coordination, can easily be abused. They may be set up unnecessarily; they are highly likely to continue to meet after the need for them has passed; they are difficult to run efficiently. Hence the value both of looking critically at all proposals for new committees in order to decide whether they can serve a useful purpose, and of reviewing at intervals whether or not existing committees are still needed.

The advantages of committees and other less formal group meetings are a guide to when they can be helpful:

1. They can improve decision-making by bringing together all those whose experience is necessary to the decision. They are a means of coordinating the different viewpoints and knowledge of departments, and so ensuring that no relevant knowledge is overlooked. It is easier to judge how strongly people feel about particular points in a group discussion than in written memoranda.

2. They can prevent decisions being taken too quickly. Mostly people would think that a committee's capacity to delay decision-taking is one of its great disadvantages, but there can be times when it is important to try and reach the best decision, even if this takes longer, and where this can best be done in a committee, rather than in an informal group.

3. Committees can have an educational value in keeping managers informed about the work of other parts of the company. However the use of committees purely for information purposes should be treated with caution; there may be less time-consuming ways of achieving the same thing. In one company, where the managers kept diaries of their activities for the author and answered daily questions about the use of their time, there were many complaints from middle managers about the amount of time wasted in large committees. Top managers said what a useful committee system they had – such a convenient method of keeping managers informed. They thought of committee meetings for information as a way of saving their time, but did not appreciate what a waste of time these meetings seemed to the middle managers.

4. Decisions made by committees are likely to be more objective than those made by an individual as there is more chance of preconceived ideas and emotional judgements being examined.

The advantages of committees have been discussed first because managers are probably aware of their disadvantages. These can be summed up briefly as follows:

1. They can slow down action, or even stifle it altogether, thus inhibiting innovation.
2. They weaken accountability because no one may feel responsible for a decision taken by a committee.
3. They take the time of a number of people, both in the actual meetings and in the paperwork before and after. For some, or all, of the people present, at least part of the meeting may be a waste of time.

A minor drawback is that it can be very difficult to find a date for a committee meeting that suits all, or even many, of the members.

What can be done to try and make the time spent in formal meetings more profitable? Dale[5] has usefully summed up some of the lessons from research and writing as follows:

1. • Composition – members should have homogeneity of outlook so that they are able to reach agreement, but heterogeneity of background so that each can make a distinctive contribution to the discussion.
   • Strong personality clashes should be avoided as they are likely to inhibit constructive discussion.
   • Ideally members should want to take a moderate part in the discussion, being neither too active not too retiring. However, there may be good reasons for not aiming at the ideal as it might mean excluding an overly talkative character who yet had an original contribution to make.
2. Subject matter – two groups of subjects are specially suitable for committees:
   • problems that have many possible solutions;
   • those that affect many aspects of the organization.
3. Size – the size that is appropriate will obviously vary with the purpose of the committee. Smaller groups are better for reaching conclusions. Bales, after experimental studies of small groups, has suggested that committees should be limited to seven members.

Whatever the composition, size and purpose of the committee, good chairmanship will make a great difference to the speed and usefulness of the discussion, as can efficient preparation of committee papers.

Another way of thinking about improving the effectiveness of formal groups, where there is some choice over group composition, is provided by Meredith Belbin. Over the years he has been developing the ideas that successful management groups – he calls them teams – need to have a mix of people who can contribute to the different tasks that have to be done. Some of the phrases that he has used to describe these, such as shaper and plant, are now familiar to many participants in management development programmes.[6]

Informal Discussions

Much coordination takes place in informal discussions, often among managers at the same level but in different departments. These discussions may happen only as the need arises, or they may be regular, though still informal. Such horizontal contacts have the advantage of causing few or no status problems; hence the people involved are likely to talk more freely to each other than to people of a different rank from themselves. In many organizations it is desirable that such discussions take place at all levels in the management hierarchy.

Coordination by informal discussions have contrasting advantages and disadvantages compared with coordination by committees. The main advantages are that they need only take place when required and only involve those who are relevant to the particular issue. They are also likely to be shorter and more informal. The disadvantages are that they may not take place and some of those who ought to be involved may not be there, either because they were not asked or were not available then. Coordination by informal discussions is less desirable where advance preparation and hence advance warning would be useful, where it is important to ensure that all relevant interests are represented and where a record of the discussion is required. Informal discussions are especially useful for smaller groups and for planning and coordinating rapid troubleshooting.

The value of facilitating informal contacts between those whose work is related is often forgotten when planning office layouts. People are most likely to talk with those they meet naturally, whether in a communal office, restaurant, lift, lavatory or corridor. They will tend to feel friendly to them; studies have shown that propinquity intensifies people's feelings for each other and that they will more often like than dislike each other.

The value of managers' dining-rooms is often recognized in companies as a means of facilitating contact, as well as a mark of status. Even those who dislike the creation of a separate dining-room for the latter reason may yet think that it is worthwhile for the former reason. But to whom is it most useful that people should talk at lunchtime? This is a relevant question in any organization and one that may need consideration when the building is designed. In companies the division, if there is one, is between levels in the hierarchy; in hospitals, for example, the division may be between nursing staff, medical staff, and others. Whatever the division, it will help to create or to perpetuate distinctions between those who eat in separate rooms. However, despite eating in the same room people often still choose to sit at the table with people from their own level or immediate work group rather than in a more mixed group.

Mid-morning coffee or afternoon tea is the recognized time when people from different departments meet together in some academic and research institutions. Interdepartmental queries tend to be raised then; it is convenient to do so, because one knows that that is when one can expect to see the people you want to talk to and because it avoids interrupting their work at other times. In hospitals the administrator and head nurse may make a practice of taking coffee together so that they can discuss any common problems. Such informal get-togethers provide the opportunity to talk about related problems but, because they are informal, they need only be used as such when necessary, and the time taken can be much more flexible than informal meetings.

Projects

The establishment of a separate group is a common method of coordinating work on a new project. The staff, including the project manager, are often seconded from other departments to work together for the duration of the project. On its completion they will probably return to their old departments. The establishment of a separate group means that its members concentrate on the project for its duration. They become members of the same unit, instead of remaining members of different departments trying to work together on a common task. Many project groups are part of a matrix organization, having the advantages and problems discussed in the last chapter.

The separate project group can be a powerful tool for ensuring coordination between people of different backgrounds. It is most suitable where there is a clear job to be done, which has a definite end and which can, therefore, provide a clear objective for members of the group. The composition of the group is important, especially if it is a small one. The members should be able to work together and should have different contributions to make.

SUMMARY

Coordination is necessary to ensure that related activities in different groups and departments mesh together and contribute to the common purpose. Wherever there is a need for coordination there is likely to be a problem in obtaining it. Problems arise from the conflicts of interest between individuals, groups and departments, and between the organization as a whole and its subdivisions. Problems come, too, from the different viewpoints of those in dissimilar jobs. There are also the difficulties caused by bad work allocation, poor grouping of activities, inadequate communications, and by inertia where coordination between public bodies is required.

Coordination problems can be reduced by good organization, but the most appropriate method will depend on the circumstances; an organization that is in a stable environment can have more formalized means of coordination than one that has to cope with rapid change, or with making one-off products.

The chain of command is a major means of coordination in many organizations. The more stable the environment the more true that is. Rapid change means that informal coordination amongst peers becomes more important. Each manager has either to try to synchronize his or her subordinates' work, if it is related, or to encourage them to do so themselves. The way in which activities are grouped will have an important effect on the amount of coordination that is needed and on the ease or difficulty with which it can be achieved. Committees, despite their disadvantages, are a useful means of coordinating the knowledge and viewpoints of different individuals and departments; anyone considering setting up a committee should be familiar with their uses and abuses and the ways in which they can be made to work best. Much coordination can be achieved by informal discussions, and thought should be given to making it easy for the people who need to talk to each other to do so. Here the physical layout and the eating arrangements are particularly important. The project group is a usual method of coordinating work on a new project.

NOTES

1. Peter M. Blau and W. Richard Scott, *Formal Organizations* (London: Routledge & Kegan Paul, 1963) pp. 127–8.
2. Herbert Kaufman, *The Forest Ranger: A Study in Administrative Behaviour* (Baltimore, Md: Johns Hopkins University Press, 1960) p. 210.
3. Ibid.
4. F. Luthans, *Organizational Behaviour* (New York: McGraw-Hill, 1981) p. 326.
5. Ernest Dale, *Organizations* (New York: American Management Association, 1967) pp. 175–6.
6. R. Meredith Belbin, *Management Teams: Why They Succeed or Fail* (Oxford: Heinemann, Professional Publishing, 1981).

Part III
Some Common
Organizational Problems

The main problems that arise in managing organizations are of three kinds. There are those that stem from relationships between individuals and groups; those that arise from trying to keep a good balance between the advantages and disadvantages of different forms of organization; and those that result from changes affecting the organization.

Some types of relationships are potentially a problem in any kind of organization. There are the problems of relations between superiors and subordinates, where effective communications up and down are often difficult to achieve. There are the problems that arise between managers and specialists which are likely to be even greater when the specialists are professionals who expect to act autonomously. Finally, there are the problems that arise in relations between managers at the same level. These three types of problems are discussed in separate chapters.

The most difficult organizational problems that arise in medium- and large-scale organizations are those of striking a balance between different organizational policies. A fourth chapter is devoted to the problem of deciding what is the right balance between the need for control, an argument for centralization, and the need to encourage initiative, an argument for decentralization. A fifth chapter considers the conflict between the need for order and that for flexibility.

The last three chapters consider different aspects of the problems of change in organizations. The first of these, 'The Changing Organization', seeks to relate changes in the environment to the changes that have taken place in organizations. Illustrations are given of the impact of these changes on a large industrial company and on a large hospital. The second, 'Changing the Organization', describes the kinds of changes that managers in companies and in the public services are trying to make in the structure of the organization and in the way it works. It discusses the lessons that can be learnt from examples of successful change. The third discusses the organizational problems of providing managers for the future.

5 Superior–Subordinate Relationships

This is a subject on which a great deal has been written and innumerable studies conducted. Much of the earlier writing and research focused on first-line supervisors and their workers. In this chapter the focus will be primarily on relations between superiors and subordinates within management and between managers and those who are employed for their brains – sometimes called 'knowledge workers'. These are the relationships that characterize most managers' jobs today rather than the management of manual and routine office workers. This chapter aims to look briefly at the problems of the superior–subordinate relationship, to describe what research has revealed about it, and to discuss how the nature of the organization can help to determine the character of this relationship. It focuses upon individual relationships rather than upon that of the superior with a group of subordinates.

The superior–subordinate relationship is the main, sometimes the only, one that is formally established by the organization. It is the one that is shown on the traditional organization chart. For most managers it is a key relationship and takes up more time than any other type of contact.

The success of the relationship between superiors and their staff will affect the efficiency of their departments. Not only is it important for the superior, but also for the subordinates, since it is likely to affect their future prospects as well as how they feel about their present job.

HOW THE SETTING AFFECTS THE RELATIONSHIP

The Cultural Background

The relationship between a superior and a subordinate does not exist in a vacuum, but in a particular cultural and organizational setting which helps to determine its character. The culture of the country, perhaps even of the locality, provides the stage for the two roles. The degree of formality or of camaraderie between the two will be influenced by the cultural pattern, as will the type of leadership. In some countries the manager will be expected to be autocratic; in other a more democratic, participative approach will be the custom, especially at the managerial level. In China during the cultural revolution managers had to spend two to three days a week in manual work; the aim was to keep them in close touch with the workers so that there was no gulf in understanding.

The differences in cultural background of different countries can provide hazards for the expatriate manager. In an Asian country, for example, a newly appointed English-factory manager wanted to establish friendly relations with his workforce. On one of his factory inspections he stopped to talk with one of the girls and to say something nice about her work. He chose one of the plainest girls so that his action should not be misinterpreted. When he was leaving the factory at the end of the day he was stopped by a seedy-looking man, who said 'You like my sister. How much?'

The Organizational Setting

The national culture sets the general expectations that people have of the relationship between superior and subordinates; within this there can be variations caused by the traditions that have grown up in the organization, the nature of the formal organization and the personalities of the individuals.

The formal organization can affect the relationship in two main ways. The first is by the span of control that it establishes. Managers with many subordinates will not be able to supervise their work as closely as those with only a few. The second is by the amount of support that it gives to the manager's formal authority. Managers may be given certain powers over their subordinates, including the right to determine, within limits, their pay increases. There may also be marks of rank and status that distinguish each level in the hierarchy.

But how far should the organization seek to support the formal authority of its managers? The most powerful weapons that it can give are the right to take disciplinary action and the right to award good performance, although in many countries managers can no longer be given the right to fire unsatisfactory employees, because of government regulations.

How useful is the other type of support for formal authority, that of marks of rank and status? The marks of rank, whether they be uniforms or the use of a title or a surname, help to create social distance between the levels in the hierarchy, as does the use of separate dining-rooms and lavatories, for examples. Social distance, in turn, means that the relations between levels are likely to be more formal and that the manager is likely to be treated with the outward marks of respect. Some managers are afraid that without these formal signs of respect their authority will be undermined. Whether managers do, in practice, lose any of their power of control over their subordinates depends upon their ability to exercise personal authority or influence. Managers who have no means, within themselves, of earning the respect and cooperation of their staff will be powerless without the formal authority of their position. Even with such power, their ability to control subordinates will be very limited – remember that subordinates have power too, if only that of passive resistance. One unpopular manager almost worked himself into the grave because his subordinates always did what he asked them to do but never did anything else – an ingenious and very effective form of working to rule. The more managers need the cooperation of staff – and the more skilled and interrelated the work, the more they *will* need it – the less they can rely on formal authority to obtain it. Social distance can thus be a handicap as it may impede the free give-and-take of information. This is one of the reasons why so many British companies have reduced the physical distinctions, like different eating and parking places, between managers and those who work for them. A study of the reactions of British workers to Japanese managers in Japanese factories in the UK found that one of the things that they preferred about Japanese managers, compared with British managers, was their more egalitarian attitude.[1]

The reader who visits other organizations might try observing the differing relations between superiors and subordinates. How much social distance is there between them? What is the explanation for differences between the various organizations? How far are they due to differences in the work, to the influence of tradition, or to particular personalities? Many ways of establishing social distance can be observed apart from formal provisions of the organization such as separate lavatories. Do subordinates sit down in the superior's room without being invited to do so? Are they introduced to callers, and how is the introduction made? These and many other examples can be noticed by an observant visitor.

The organization can have other influences upon the relationship between superior and subordinate apart from those that are formally established. Kahn and his colleagues[2] in the United States suggest that there are five types of organizational behaviour that seem to be characteristic of the organization rather than of particular individuals or jobs:

1. the extent to which the individual is expected to obey rules and follow orders;
2. the extent to which superiors are expected to show a personal interest in and to nurture their subordinates;
3. the extent to which all relationships are conducted according to general rather than individual standards;

4. how detailed supervision is expected to be;
5. the extent to which organization members are expected to strive actively for achievement and advancement.

This list is a description of some of the codes of behaviour that exist in an organization, and which are often called its culture. The culture of an organization has a powerful influence on the relationship between superiors and subordinates. The five points above are particularly relevant to the superior–subordinate relationship.

PROBLEMS OF THE RELATIONSHIP

One aspect of the relationship that can cause problems is mutual dependence. They need each other if they are to succeed. Each can help or handicap the other. Superiors are dependent upon their subordinates because they are accountable for their subordinates' performance. The subordinate is dependent upon the boss: how dependent will vary with the job and the organization. In any job the boss's good opinion is likely to matter for advancement and now in many organizations for ratings for performance-related pay. In some jobs the subordinate may also be dependent upon the boss for resources, for the amount of freedom to use his or her own judgement and for access to information that is needed to do the job well. Dependence can cause frictions. These frictions are likely to be greater if either, and particularly the subordinates had problems in adjusting to their parents. They may carry some of those past tensions into their relationship with their boss, because this is another authority figure to be rebelled against.

From the Superior's Point of View

Superiors have to decide how they should divide the work between themselves and their subordinates. This means that they must decide what should be delegated and to whom. Delegation has three aspects to it. First is the assigning of tasks to particular subordinates. Next is giving them the authority to carry out these tasks, which includes the means for doing so, and last is making them responsible for those tasks. Although managers should hold subordinates responsible for the work delegated to them, it does not lessen their own responsibility for the efficiency of their unit. In some jobs, such as the regional director for a group of retail chain stores, the tasks at each level are laid down by top management so there are no, or very few, decisions to be made about delegation.

The main problem for managers, though they may not realize it, lies in knowing what they should do themselves. The first decision is what should be done because of the managers' position. Managers will have more power than their subordinates, and this can obviously be important with some types of contact. Managers will also have a representative role for their group, for example as managing director of the company or as head of their department, and there will thus be some jobs that they alone should do. Additionally, they will need to concern themselves with the more important policy decisions affecting their command, and not be so preoccupied with day-to-day matters that they do not have time for this. They should create and maintain a climate that encourages their subordinates to work well. Finally, they must retain the overall responsibility for checking on the work of their command. These are the jobs they should do because of their position in the hierarchy. There may be other tasks that they think they can do better than their staff, but such decisions are fraught with the dangers of self-deception and the natural desire to continue doing work that they enjoy rather than the perhaps less congenial, but more appropriate, work for their position.

Managers should remember that, although they can more easily get information from the managers at their own level than from their subordinates, the latter may more readily get information from their peers. In a large organization, interdepartmental relations may be much franker among junior managers than they are higher up. Managers should therefore recognize that their staff may be in a better position than they are to find out what is happening.

Once they have decided what they ought to be doing and what work they should delegate to subordinates, managers can then turn to the problem of how to divide the delegated work amongst their staff. They may be influenced by the classical writers, who talk of equating authority and responsibility, but this implies that the work can be divided into neat parcels, one for each job. In practice, the work may be such that it will be done best if the staff act as a team. Even if the work can be parcelled out, managers may think that it is undesirably restrictive to give their staff specifically defined responsibilities. Sometimes they may not understand enough about their subordinates' work to do so, even if they wanted to; this may well be the position of managers who are responsible for a new type of specialist, or those who have subordinates trained in a different discipline from their own.

Next, managers must be able to tell their staff what they want done, as well as be willing to listen and able to understand what it is they say about the work.[3] The first essential when explaining what one wants done – and this is where many managers fail – is to be sufficiently clear in one's own mind about what one wants. Managers should make clear to their subordinates what they expect of them. How far they should spell out these expectations will depend in part upon the stability of the work that has to be done and in part upon the ability and experience of the staff. New or poorly trained staff will need more detail than those who are experienced. In a relatively stable situation the superior should be able to describe clearly what are the objectives, how they should be achieved and how their achievement should be measured; in more fluid situations a group exploration of what needs doing and of how to do it may be more fruitful than prescriptions from the superior. Even in relatively stable situations the superior will gain more commitment to achieving the objectives if these are agreed rather than imposed.

Managers must know whether they and their staff speak a common language, as those with a common professional training should do, or whether they must make allowances for misunderstandings that can arise from different backgrounds. A more difficult barrier to communication stems from the superior-subordinate relationship itself. Each is likely to tell the other what they want to communicate rather than what the other wants to hear. Some superiors can inspire sufficient confidence to reduce this barrier greatly, but few are likely to overcome it altogether.

A traditional task of managers is 'motivation' – getting people to perform effectively. Leavitt distinguishes different ways of doing this: by the use of formal authority, that is by formal power; by coercive power; by manipulation; and by a shared collaborative activity.[4] A superior who relies on formal authority is narrowing the effective range of control over others. The advantages of using authority are that it imposes orderliness and conformity – simplifying the problems of coordination and control; it is simpler to use authority, because it is generally understood, whereas if one wants to use persuasion one must understand the motivations of the individual one is seeking to persuade. Authority is faster as time is not taken up with explanations. Finally, some people enjoy exercising authority and like the demonstrations of respect that it may produce. The disadvantages of using authority are that it may not only produce unintended reactions, such as a mere show of conformity or even an atmosphere of distrust and hostility, but it may also reduce the possibilities for future communication and hence undermine the superior's ability to influence the subordinates – Leavitt calls this the 'irreversibility of restrictive methods'. In general, he suggests that formal authority is more used, and more useful, at the lower levels of the hierarchical pyramid though that is less true today than in the past. At the managerial level it is a change of attitude rather than of actions that is wanted, and this is more likely to be achieved by influence through collaboration rather than by exercising formal authority.

Leavitt's second method of influencing people is by the exercise of coercive power – threatening retaliation unless the person does what is wanted. He describes this as 'blackmail, pressure, threat – the power tactic that almost all of us despise, and almost all of us use'. He also usefully reminds us that 'the line between "coercive" and "normal" persuasion sometimes becomes very fine. The "brain-washing" that most of us deplore is in principle not very different from the "education" that most of us positively value.'[5]

His third method is manipulation. Again, this is a method used by most people, although they might not accept that they do so. A denial of using manipulation may be followed by the statement that, to get people to accept a change, you should make them think that the idea is theirs. This is a common example, as is much salesmanship, of trying to influence people without telling them of your real motives; instead, you try to build up a relationship of trust. Leavitt concludes that, in many situations, manipulation is a useful method and, 'by most standards, moral'. Yet we should remain aware of its dangers, particularly of undermining trust.

The fourth method is that of trying to influence people by encouraging them to take responsibility for the change themselves. The process thus becomes a more collaborative one. It underlies much of the discussion about the need to change the culture of an organization. 'You have', as one chief executive explained, 'to persuade people of the justice of your cause [he was talking about the changes being made to achieve a turnaround] and get them to share your belief and your sense of doing things.'

There are yet other methods of getting people to perform effectively than the four described by Leavitt. There are all the methods that make up what the Americans call the 'remuneration package'. Yet another method of influencing people is by encouraging the development of peer pressure, which can be a by-product of a successfuly communicated need to improve efficiency. As one chief executive put it: 'I guess that survival of the fittest takes over. They begin themselves, in their locally based teams to identify and isolate weak links – and it doesn't need me to do it, which is very pleasing.'

Managers may need to check to see that what they wanted done has been done. This raises problems of what methods of control to use, how technically efficient they are, and how they will be seen by their staff. At one extreme, staff may view attempts of control as imposed, unreasonable, and to be circumvented whenever possible. At the other extreme, they may view them as targets that they suggested and that have been mutually agreed and reviewed. The setting of mutually agreed objectives is one approach to trying to provide an acceptable framework for control. It is a formalized method of identifying and defining goals and targets that is then linked to performance assessment.

At a more general level, we find that the problem areas in the relationship between superior and subordinate have remained the same, but the character of the relationship has changed with time. Circumstances have made the boss a less authoritarian figure than in the past. The higher level of education and the more democratic character of society have made an autocratic manner old-fashioned, while the decreasing value of experience compared with up-to-date knowledge has reduced superiors' authority in many organizations. They are thus less likely to be able to dictate what ought to be done, and instead may have to ask their subordinate's advice as to what should be done. Older managers may well feel worried and insecure as they hear their staff talking about things that they themselves do not understand, although this is less of a problem than it used to be, with more managers attending post-experience courses and the atmosphere in many organizations being freer than in the past.

A further problem for some superiors is that they are too anxious to be liked by their staff – a characteristic of some British managers, but not of some of their European neighbours, who are more interested in being respected. This anxiety may make some British managers reluctant to criticize for fear their subordinates may resent it.

The superior's job can be a lonely one, though this is truest for those at the top and for those on the first rung. The former can be in an isolated position with no peers in the organization; the latter, if they have been promoted from the shopfloor, will have lost the camaraderie of their workmates without becoming real members of the management team.

From the Subordinate's Point of View

Superiors may feel that the problems are all on their side, but that is not how many subordinates would see the relationship. Today, especially, the answers of many to the question 'What problems are there in your work?' would include 'Managing the boss'. Subordinates' attitudes to their superiors are likely to be ambivalent. They may enjoy dependence, as many people do, feeling relieved to have somebody else whose job it is to cope in a crisis and who takes the final rap. However, they are also likely to resent the relationship, especially if they feel that they are working for somebody who they think is incompetent or out of date. Of course, they may just resent the mere fact of being subordinate, even where they respect their superiors.

Another of the subordinate's problems is that of trying to please the boss. According to American research, most managers, at least in the United States, tend to be upward-orientated. They care more about what their superior thinks of them than they do about what their subordinates think of them. However, this may vary with their career stage. Ambitious young managers are more likely to care about their superiors' views of them, while older managers may be more interested in their subordinates. There is also, according to a study of 113 American managers in a wide variety of companies, a difference between line and staff managers.[6] The latter are more prone than the former to trying to influence their superiors to provide them with benefits, to think well of them and to help them in their work. This difference can probably be explained by the more intangible, and hence less easily evaluated, nature of staff compared with line jobs.

Subordinates often complain that they cannot please their manager because they do not know what is wanted. This can happen because the superiors do not know themselves what they want, or because they have not explained their demands clearly.

The discussion so far has assumed that the subordinate has only one superior. However, as we shall discuss in the next chapter, she may have both a line superior to whom she is responsible and a staff one to whom she is responsible for her professional standards. She may also be given instructions by her superior's superior, and come into contact with those senior to her whose requests she may feel it impolitic to refuse. She may, therefore, have multiple relationships with a variety of senior managers. Such a situation can lead to stress, particularly if the various instructions and requests are at variance with those of her immediate superior. However, the ambitious employee may well welcome the opportunity to be visible to other senior managers.

LEADERSHIP STYLE

This heading describes a central preoccupation of the human relations school, particularly in the United States, where many research workers have explored how performance is affected by the way a person leads. This is not a subject that interested the classical school of management writers; although they described motivation as one of the tasks of management, they did not ask themselves research-type questions like 'What happens if the boss is autocratic?' or 'What is the effect of a manager who encourages staff to participate in decision-making?'

What has reasearch shown about the effectiveness of different types of leadership? The original centre of this investigation from 1947 on was at the Institute of Social Research at the University of Michigan in the United States, under the leadership of Rensis Likert. The findings, from a study of a wide variety of different types of large organizations, showed that the best performance is obtained by leadership that is employee-centred. This means that leaders think first of the employees' welfare and only second of production, and that they supervise in a general rather than in a close, detailed way.[7] Such findings encouraged some of the members of the human relations school in the United States to emphasize the value of participative management, two-way communication and permissive leadership.

The universal applicability of these findings was later questioned by a number of other studies, which showed that the leadership style should vary with the situation and with the people concerned. It is now generally accepted that there is no one best leadership style. What is best will depend on the circumstances, and these may vary in different parts of the organization as well as from one organization to another. In some organizations, or parts of the organization, initiative will be important, while in others the punctual performance of prescribed duties may be what matters. For example, a research and development department, where the need is for innovation, seems to require a participative and egalitarian leadership style. This contrasts with the work of the production department, where the greater need for short-term results requires a more directive style of leadership.

What should be cheering to the manager is that observation shows that many different styles of leadership work. One may be preferable to another in a particular setting, but if it is alien to the manager's personality he is unlikely to make a better leader by trying to change his style radically.

Of course, difficulties may still arise when subordinates have to adjust to a new boss with a different style. Some may be unable to do so, especially if they have adapted successfully over a long time to a radically different style. It may be as hard to adjust to a participative boss, who expects subordinates to show initiative, after working with an autocratic boss, who expected subordinates to do only what they had been told, as vice versa.

From the mid-1980s there has been a greatly renewed interest in leadership. It is the subject of many books written for managers.[8] Leadership is now seen as more important than in the past because of the need to transform so many organizations in business and the public sector. Radical change requires leadership if subordinates, and colleagues, are to accept and be attracted by the leader's view of the way forward. This view may not originate with the leader but he or she must be able to symbolize its importance. Leaders, unlike managers, point the way and encourage others to follow.

SUMMARY

The main focus of the chapter has been on supervisory relations, both within management and between managers and knowledge workers.

The superior-subordinate relationship is formally established by the organization. For most managers it takes up more time than any other form of contact. It is a vital relationship for both parties.

It is affected by its cultural and organizational environment, which sets the general expectations of behaviour. The formal organization also influences the relationship by the span of control that it establishes and by the amount of support that it gives to the manager's formal authority.

The problems of the relationship were looked at first from the point of view of the superior and then from that of the subordinate. Superiors must decide what work they should do themselves and what they should delegate. They have to motivate their staff to do what they want. They can do so by using their authority, by coercion, by manipulation and by influence. They can provide the framework for assessing achievement by establishing agreed objectives. Subordinates are likely to have ambivalent feelings about their boss. One of their problems may be trying to educate the boss to understand the problems; another may be trying to please him or her.

Much human relations research in the United States has studied the effects of different styles of leadership. The earlier research showed that the best performance is obtained by employee-centred leadership and by general rather than close, detailed supervision. Later research indicated that there is no one best style; what is best in a particular instance will depend upon the nature of the work and upon the needs of the people being supervised. However, this can cause difficulties when departmental members who are led in very different ways have to work with each other. The transformation needed in so many organizations in business and the public sector makes leadership more important today. Leaders are those who can show the way forward and encourage others to follow.

NOTES

1. Michael White and Malcolm Trevor, *Under Japanese Management: The Experience of British Workers* (London: Heinemann, Policy Studies Institute, 1983).
2. R. L. Kahn and others, *Organizational Stress: Studies in Role, Conflict and Ambiguity* (New York: John Wiley, 1964). Quoted in D. Katz and R. L. Kahn, *The Social Psychology of Organizations* (New York: John Wiley, 1964) p. 192.

3. The problems of communications, and the barriers to it, are discussed in many books. Harold J. Leavitt has a useful discussion in *Managing Behaviour in Organizations*, 5th edn (Chicago, Ill.: University of Chicago Press, 1988) ch. 8.

4. Ibid., chs 10–13

5. Ibid., pp. 137–8.

6. Stuart M. Schmidt and David Kipnis, 'Managers' Pursuit of Individual and Organizational Goals', *Human Relations*, vol. 37, no. 10 (October 1984).

7. Rensis Likert, *New Patterns of Management* (New York: McGraw-Hill, 1961).

8. In the UK, John Harvey-Jones, *Making it Happen: Reflections on Leadership* (London: Collins, 1988) was possibly the start of his new career as a management guru after being a successful chief executive of ICI.

6 The Manager and the Specialist

A perennial problem in organizations is how to make the best use of people who provide specialist aid to managers of the main core activities. In older books on management this was discussed as line and staff authority relationships. The distinction between line and staff is rarer today because it is often less clear-cut. However, many of the traditional problems of making the best use of specialist roles remain. They are too often seen as new problems because of the variety of new jobs and of new organizational relationships. Instead, they should be seen as new versions of old problems so that use can be made of past experience. The aim of this chapter is to analyse the kinds of problems that arise in the relations between managers of the main activities and specialists and to discuss what can be done to reduce them.

The phrase 'line and staff' is still used in some organizations, despite the confusion that it can cause. Because of this the words are used occasionally in this chapter where they would be used by many managers, particularly when talking of reporting to two bosses or of providing varied job experience. 'Line manager' is most commonly used to refer to someone who is in charge of operations, while 'staff' is used for those who provide specialist expertise, whose output is information.

The traditional staff roles, such as personnel – now often enlarged into human resource management – continue, but often new roles are being created. The sudden growth of particular new posts can be seen as a response to a new organizational need or, to the more cynically inclined, as a reflection of a current fashion – the latest panacea for organizational ills. These posts may spring up in a wide variety of organizations – quality manager is a recent example – or they may be specific to particular organizations. An example of the latter was the establishment in 1987 in ICI of business engineers within the corporate ICI engineering group. The aim of this new specialist group was to provide a better link between the central engineering group and the individual businesses. A by-product of the organizational changes in the NHS from 1990 provides another example of the growth of new specialist posts with titles such as health promotion manager, health outcomes officer, occupational health audit facilitator, HIV prevention coordinator and business development manager. Often new specialists have the task of seeking to influence others, mainly line management, to take more account of their subject area.

DIFFERENT ORGANIZATIONAL RELATIONSHIPS BETWEEN MANAGERS AND SPECIALISTS

The nature of the problems that arise between managers and specialists vary with their organizational relationships. The specialist may be as follows:

1. on the staff of the manager, and with no other organizational link;
2. on the staff of the manager, but with a functional relationship to a more senior member of the speciality;
3. in a separate department. These departments can be distinguished by the nature of their relationship with the other departments:
   - they are purely service departments;
   - their task is solely to advise management;
   - they have some authority to determine policy as well as to advise;
   - they audit or inspect the work of other departments.
4. the specialist is outside the organization and is employed as a consultant.

Specialist is on the Manager's Staff

The simplest relationship is the first listed above, where the specialist is on the manager's staff and has no other organizational link. This relationship has become more common in slimmed-down organizations as service functions, such as maintenance and production control in a manufacturing company, are put under the production manager's control rather than in separate service departments. Even this relationship can be difficult, particularly for older managers who have worked their way up from the bottom and who are unused to the new speciality. In the days when knowledge increased fairly slowly, a manager would become more expert as a result of experience. Hence managers could be looked up to because they were likely to know more. The speeding-up of technological change has altered this.

There are new specialities, and much expansion and sub-division of old ones, which the manager may know little or nothing about. The old saying 'Knowledge itself is power' applies to the organizational hierarchy;

subordinates who have specialist knowledge not shared by their bosses will have more power than their colleagues whose training is in the same field as that of their boss.

Today managers may have to work with subordinates whose speciality they know little or nothing about. This can create problems, arising partly from their own attitudes and those of their subordinates and partly from their inability to manage something that they do not understand. The differences in attitude between managers and specialists will be discussed at a later stage. Here it is worth pointing out that managers should not abdicate their responsibilities: they should train staff to put forward their proposals in as simple a way as possible and describe the nature of the choice in language that they can understand; they should concern themselves with the logic of the proposals and learn to ask questions that can help to test this.

Specialist Reports to Two Bosses

The second relationship listed above occurs where a specialist, such as a maintenance engineer, reports not only to a manager, usually called the line boss, who is responsible for *what* is done and when it is done, but also to a specialist superior outside the department, usually called the staff boss, who is responsible for *how* it is done. The task of the staff boss is thus to maintain professional standards. For example, common procedures may be established for the organization: the chief accountant may specify the form in which accounts are to be kept and the chief engineer may specify maintenance procedures.

The problems of the specialist reporting to a line manager, but also having what is called a 'functional' responsibility to a staff boss, are obvious. They stem from the dual allegiance, from the possibility that subordinates may be given conflicting instructions by two bosses, and the likelihood that they may pay more attention to one boss than to the other – probably the one they think is most important in furthering their careers. Problems are inevitable when an individual has two bosses, but they can be diminished by appropriate action and attitudes.

Important for the success of this relationship are the attitudes of the subordinate and the two managers. The subordinate should have integrity, and not play one boss off against the other. The line and staff bosses should understand the demands of each other's work and seek to ensure that both contribute to the organization's objectives, instead of playing politics or thinking too narrowly in terms of their own departments. This description of desirable attitudes immediately shows how difficult it can be to achieve a satisfactory relationship. Important, too, is the organizational clarity of the relationship, so that subordinates know to whom they are responsible for what – in many companies subordinates are not made aware of this.

Specialist is in a Separate Department

The third organizational relationship between the manager and the specialist is where the latter is in a separate department. These departments must be distinguished according to the tasks they perform and the ways in which these impinge on the manager.

The simplest relationship with other departments is where the specialist provides a service that managers have to use; catering is a good example. The transport department can also come into this category. In these examples managers may grumble about the service they get, but there will be none of the other difficulties found in relations between managers and specialists.

In contrast, there are other types of specialist departments where the relationship between user and provider is more difficult. These are the departments providing a service, such as training, which managers may not have to use. The department must then sell its services, either literally in some companies, or in the sense of persuading managers to use them in others. The relationship between specialists and managers here is like that of seller and customer, with the former anxious to please and the latter perhaps sceptical, perhaps concerned, about how they can find out whether the service being offered is really worthwhile. Managers are unlikely to be perturbed by this type of relationship with the specialist, though, like any customer, there is always the danger that they may become disillusioned with what they have been sold. The specialists are more likely to have problems, particularly as they may suffer from frustration if they feel that the value of their services is not adequately recognized.

Additionally, specialists can do more than advise or provide a service. They may also be given authority to issue instructions on particular subjects, this 'functional authority' being usually concerned with how things should be done. When specialists are given such authority over particular policies or procedures, its extent and nature should be clearly stated so as to prevent ambiguity about their power to issue instructions. The danger of functional authority is that it reduces the scope of the manager's job. This is much less of a problem than in the past with the decline in the number and size of central staff departments. However, it still exists in some large organizations particularly in the public sector. Kaufman's classic study of the forest ranger in the US Forest Service illustrates the problems that can still arise where there are central staff departments:

the instructions field officers are called upon to execute are not always easily reconciled . . . The specifications for roads, for example, are generally predicated on engineering premises alone, but roads built to those specifications may conflict with the demands of watershed management or recreation management or timber management specialists . . . Emphasis on recreation that gratifies recreation officers may disturb fire control officers. What looks like adequate concern for the grazing uses of the national forests may seem like indifference to wildlife management from the perspective of those who specialize in this function. Administrative assistants call for greater attention to office routines and procedures and paperwork, while other functional specialists deplore expenditures of Ranger time in the office rather than in the woods. Despite the general consensus on the desirability of multiple-use management, it is not always clear what this indicates in specific instances.[1]

The geographical separation which is a feature of the US Forest Service is also found in many large organizations. This adds to the problems, in that the specialists may have difficulty in appreciating local conditions, thus increasing the risk of conflicting instructions from different departments. The specialist departments in large organizations may be at head or divisional offices, which can further complicate the relationship between the specialists and the managers who are in local units; the specialists are liable to become identified by local management with the 'They' who do not understand the reality of operating conditions.

Specialist is an Outsider

This situation is much more common than in the past. It is one managerial response to the need for greater flexibility in using people. Contracting out work cuts down on expensive overheads and means that specialist aid will only be paid for when there is a demand for it. Another reason for the greater use of external specialists is that many organizations have found that it can be more economic to use companies which specialize in providing that particular service. The service may also be of a higher standard because it is the core activity of the company providing it. The move to buying-in services started in commercial companies but many public-sector organizations have been under strong political pressure to do so too.

These are the reasons why external specialists are now used more frequently. There are also the long-standing reasons for using them, for example, small companies, as well as large companies that need highly specialized advice, may not have enough work to justify employing their own specialist staff; the occasional or part-time use of outside specialists is therefore more economic. Companies may also use outsiders because the best specialists may not be attracted to full-time appointments. Outsiders may be able to contribute more because they have had experience of other organizations; top management may want to have an outside opinion so that it is not entirely dependent upon the advice of its own specialists; top management may also find it is easier to talk to an outsider because there is not the reticence on either side that can come from a difference in hierarchical levels. While top management may be loath to admit ignorance to a subordinate or to ask questions that may seem foolish, they may be happy to do so with an outsider. Top management may also learn from the outsider what questions they should be asking their own specialists.

There is another, and quite different, reason for using outside specialists: to provide an adequate reason for initiating changes which top management know should be made but cannot otherwise bring themselves to make. The advice of an outside specialist, particularly if he or she is highly paid, gives a plausible pretext for doing so.

There are dangers in the use of outside specialists, of course. Because their careers are less likely to be affected if their advice is shown to be poor, they may not be so responsible in their advice. Management, too, tends to be less critical of the recommendations of outside experts. Another danger is that very expensive external consultants may be used when they are not necessary or because it has become fashionable to do so. The expansion in the use of search consultants is an example of the latter, as shown in the claim by a chairman of an NHS Health Authority: 'We must use one because otherwise our job will not be seen as important enough. Look at the job advertisements and you will see that the better jobs all carry the byline of a firm of search consultants.'

Using outside specialists can make for greater clarity in the relationship with managers and thus reduce many of the problems that arise in the use of internal specialists. There are likely to be fewer tensions in the relationship between line management and the external specialist than in those with internal specialists. However, few relationships are trouble-free and distinctive problems arise in the use of external services. One is coordinating across a number of subcontractors: this problem is at its most intense on a complex construction site. One construction manager described how he tried to reduce the quarrels between the different specialist subcontractors over who was to blame for what went wrong, by setting up a regular risk review session. It was an informal review meeting of what had gone wrong attended by a leader from each of the subcontracting groups; there were no minutes, no notes and no tape recorders so that people would be encouraged to be frank about what had happened. Fortunately, most managers do not have such a complex set of relationships with subcontractors to manage.

A more general problem is recognizing that relations with external workers have to be managed too and that this is different from managing internal relationships. The manager has to learn how to establish an appropriate contract, especially how to define output and quality standards. There may often be an element of negotiation in using internal specialists but negotiating skills become much more important when dealing with external specialists. Motivation also matters in making effective use of them. The contract will not guarantee motivation but, particularly where it is hard to assess the quality of the service, the specialist's interest and personal commitment needs to be enlisted.

CHANGES IN RELATIONSHIP: ILLUSTRATION FROM IT AND PERSONNEL

The changes in the organizational position of the IT specialist provides a good example of the merits and snags of each of the four organizational relationships described above. It also illustrates how different organizational choices can be appropriate at different stages in the development of a new speciality. The early computer specialists were often part of the chief accountant's department. One advantage of this arrangement was that it gave them a base in a department where there was a clear need for their services. It also helped to educate the accountants in the use of computers and in recognizing what computer specialists could contribute. One disadvantage was that their location meant that their acceptance by other functions was delayed; another was that it gave them few opportunities to learn about the workings of other departments. A group of specialists who were potentially of use to a number of functions were thus in danger of being restricted by their organizational location. On balance it can be argued that putting them in the finance department was a good solution to the problem of locating a new and little-understood group of specialists.

Some years later a more common organizational solution was to set up a separate department. This could be a computing department alone or computing could be grouped with O&M to form a management services department. This overcame the disadvantages described above and gave the new specialists more potential power than they had as a subdivision of another function. It also improved their opportunities for developing computing as

a service to the organization. The emerging disadvantages were that: promises often outran performance – a particular danger in a rapidly developing
new technology; costs escalated; computer staff saw their future in new and
larger projects rather than in learning about the business and moving to
other departments; and a large gap often developed between the thinking
and understanding of the computer specialists and that of line management.

Common reactions to these disadvantages were either to use computer
bureaux or to hive off the management services department as a separate
business which then had to sell its services; this could be as an internal service department or even as a separate company. A disadvantage of an internal IT business was that it could meet its goals and increase 'profits' by
exploiting the rest of the organization who were, or felt they were, a cap-
tive market. The advantages of using external specialists were that this
could save costs and improve the motivation of the IT specialists to produce work that was valued by the commissioning managers. The major disadvantage was that external IT specialists found it harder to understand the
work of the organization and how it actually operated, hence how best to
facilitate the implementation of new systems. Therefore, using external
specialists places greater demands on line management to understand what
they need and what the systems can contribute.

Technical changes in computing and the development of information
technology opened up other organizational choices. In the days of very
large, very expensive computers which needed special rooms to house
them it was logical to have data processing as a central activity. The development of personal computers and IT networks made a much more decentralized approach both possible and often desirable. So the organizational
changes that have taken place in the position of IT have been only partly a
reaction to the emerging disadvantages of the current organizational location; they have also been much affected by the major technical changes that
have taken place.

As information technology has developed three different activities
within it have emerged more clearly: technical services to users; data processing; and systems development. These different activities need not have
the same organizational solution. It is the third one that still creates the
most difficulties.

John Dearden[2] argued in 1987 – which is quite a long time ago in the rapidly developing world of IT – that within the next five years users would
completely control individual systems, and that systems development would
be done by outside software specialists, because they would be cheaper and
better than companies' own departments. Like many predictions about the
future of computers, development has been much slower. Dearden saw one

exception to his prediction: companies with large information systems capabilities, such as financial service, insurance, automobile and airline companies. These he predicted would establish independent profit centres or subsidiaries competing both inside and outside the company to supply specialized information systems: a prediction which is coming true.

A counter-argument to Dearden's view of systems development being done by outside software specialists is that it will not capitalize on the potential of IT to change the ways things are done within organizations. To realize that potential it is vital that IT thinking is integrated into strategic thinking about the future of the organization, which means integrating the people and the function into the mainstream of the organization.

One continuing problem in the relationship between managers and IT specialists has been the gap in understanding between them. The greater computer-literacy of many managers has helped to reduce this problem, but it still remains. The gap comes now more from the need for IT managers to have a better understanding of the nature of the business; there has always been a need for them to have a greater sensitivity to the problems and choices in the implementation of new IT systems. One suggestion for closing the gap is the development of a hybrid manager who has the diverse abilities that are required: a manager who combines technical knowledge with an understanding of the particular organization and of its context.[3]

The history of changes in the organizational location of information systems is a special case of the problems of relationships between managers and specialists. It is special because of the great and continuing changes in the technology, the escalating cost of information systems and their ability to influence the working of the organization. Because information systems have become such a major and costly aspect of many organizations it has become even more important than in other specialities for the relationship problems to be reduced if not solved. However, the problems that arise in the relationship and the means of overcoming them are similar to those that arise, though often in a less acute form, in other specialities.

The personnel manager is another example of a specialist role where the relationship with line management has changed over time, as has the title, which is now more commonly 'human resource manager'. The services that the human resource manager is expected to provide have changed with, for example, more emphasis on management development, performance review and performance-related pay and less on industrial relations. There is more emphasis now on the duty of the line manager to be the people manager and for the personnel specialist to provide mainly technical knowledge and support. This change was described by the works manager of a large plant:

You have to be pretty aware of what is going on on the shop floor. My labour relations manager is there to advise, not to do the job for me. If the trade unions think it is being run by a professional labour relations person you are dead. I see him as a necessary evil. My measure of success on labour relations is when I get his department down to about two. Line managers cannot be seen to opt out. So every labour relations issue all the way down is fronted by the line manager responsible.

SOME SPECIALISTS ARE MORE ACCEPTABLE THAN OTHERS

A large organization will employ many different types of specialists who will have quite different tasks to perform. McGregor distinguished between the policeman and the professional helper and said that the two were incompatible.[4]

Inspectors and auditors clearly belong to the policeman class and will usually be treated as such. Some staff people, such as the safety officer, may have both functions. However, wherever there is a policeman element, this is likely to make it harder for the person to be seen as a helper; the tendency will be for evasion rather than cooperation.

The distinction between policeman and professional helper, though important, is not the only one that should be made. There are many different kinds of helper. For example, there are those whose task is to try to improve the efficiency of management. This is likely to be interpreted by managers as a criticism of the way in which they are working, and relations will be potentially difficult; the specialists will therefore have to try to persuade line managers that they really have something to contribute that will help them to meet their objectives. First the holders of a new specialist role need to be clear themselves about why their job exists. This is often one of the problems of getting a specialist post accepted as useful. Then they really must have something to contribute and be able to sell this to line management, who are likely to be sceptical.

Specialists, particularly those in new posts, can easily become frustrated because their attempts to help are not welcome or understood. This is particularly likely to happen where specialists are appointed to alert managers to aspects of their job that have become more important and to which they are either unable or unwilling to give the necessary attention. Such a brief may well be resented, ignored if possible or even remain unrecognized. This can be true of quality managers, except that many of them have been supported by the need in many organizations to achieve official certification of quality by means of British Standard 5750.

The reaction of managers to the different specialists will be affected, too, by their opinion of the nature of the speciality and by their recognition of the need for advice. This is illustrated in Figure 6.1, which also suggests how different specialities are likely to be viewed, though this will vary with the ability of the particular specialist. The position of the human resource manager, for example, in some organizations will be lower on each axis. The traditional professions are much more easily accepted than the newer specialities. The contribution that professional training can make is known and accepted; managers are unlikely to feel any resentment at being given advice by a lawyer, doctor or accountant, since they will not think that such advice is a reflection on their own competence or that it reduces the scope of their job. Lawyers are, perhaps, the most acceptable profession. Newer specialities, however, may receive neither respect nor acceptance. These specialities are now striving to establish the qualifications that will enable them to be accepted as professionals, and their efforts are being gradually rewarded by a growth of acceptance.

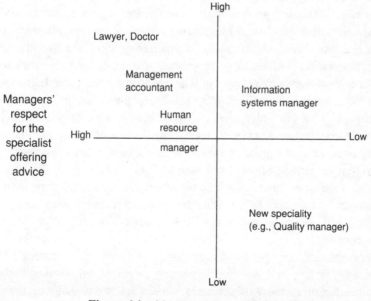

Figure 6.1 *Managers' Assessment of the Value of the Advice of Different Specialists*

THROUGH THE OTHERS' EYES

The criticisms that managers make of specialists and that specialists make of managers recur so frequently that one can describe a stereotype of the manager, or the specialist, that will be recognizable to members of the other group in most, perhaps in all, organizations.

Managers may see the specialist as impractical and out of touch with operational realities – theorists, incapable of putting their theories into practice. Even when asked for advice, they may be accused of being slow, perfectionist and vague, whereas the manager wants clear advice provided quickly; hence the old joke about the manager who asked for a one-armed economist who could not say, 'On the one hand this, and on the other hand that'. Managers may complain, too, that the specialists are trying to usurp their authority.

The specialists' picture of managers is often of reactionaries, unwilling to change and turning down suggestions that would obviously improve the efficiency of their departments. They may think of them as touchy and pre-occupied with their status; they are likely to see them as inefficient and in great need of their help, a fact which the managers will obdurately refuse to recognize. Even if they do, they are unlikely to know how to ask the right questions.

The two groups are likely to have different views of what they think is important. Specialist groups will probably attach greater importance to high quality than will line management. The latter may merely want something that works and which can be provided as quickly and cheaply as possible. Specialists will be more interested in the quality of workmanship, both because they get greater satisfaction from exercising their professional skills and because they may value the opinion of their professional colleagues, who will judge them by the quality of what they do. Hence the architect may be more interested in the appearance of a building than in its utility or its cost; the operational researcher may be preoccupied with producing an elegant solution rather than with providing something that will deal with the problem as rapidly as possible. The manager who wishes to attract and retain specialists who are in short supply, such as systems people, will need to understand their viewpoint and to make some allowance for it.

Many professional people are committed to a lifetime's career in their speciality. Their professional goals stress increased knowledge and skill and the solution of more difficult problems. These can clash with the organization's need to have the more humdrum professional work performed;

for example, the hernia operations in hospitals and the basic undergraduate teaching in universities.

The jobs of the two are also different, and this affects their attitudes. These differences show themselves in quite simple things like the pattern of the working day. Managers' days are likely to be much more fragmented than that of the specialist. The former have to deal with a wide variety of subjects and people, often for very short periods. In consequence they will find it hard to plan their day or to find a quiet period for thinking about a problem. Specialists are likely to deal with fewer subjects in a day or a week and to have fewer interruptions. They may find it hard to understand why the manager does not take time to analyse a problem.

IMPROVING RELATIONS BETWEEN MANAGERS AND SPECIALISTS

McGregor has a helpful discussion on how to improve collaboration between managers and specialists, which remains as true today as when it was written in 1960.[5] His central consideration is that the appropriate role for specialists is to provide professional help to all levels of management – the relationship should be that of consultant–client. The specialists' responsibility to all levels of management must be recognized, so staff groups should not be given responsibilities which entail their exercising authority over lower levels of management. McGregor attaches importance to managers practising self-control, so specialists should supply control data to the manager of the unit rather than to the superior.

It is specialists in central departments who are likely to cause most problems in their relationships with operational managers. The other organizational relationships discussed earlier can all help to reduce the difficulties that arise in relations between managers and specialists. A specialist on the manager's staff will get personally involved in the department's work, can get to know its problems at first hand, and is likely to be accepted as a colleague instead of being seen as an outsider – one of 'Them'. Another advantage is that the managers' authority is not reduced by the presence of specialists outside the department whose advice they may not feel able to ignore and whose rules they are expected to abide by. Because of these advantages it is worth considering whether specialists should be assigned to a manager's staff, but this is not always practical and may be costly. Specialists, too, may need to have an additional staff boss who can supervise their professional competence.

Another organizational method of easing relations is to create a specialist unit which only provides a service if asked and if paid for. This has the advantage of leaving the initiative, or at least the decision as to use of the specialist's services, to the manager. It also encourages the specialists to try to discover what the customer needs, or wants – which may be different. It has the disadvantage that the managers who may most need the services are the ones who are least likely to use them. Further, when the services have to be paid for there may be accounting problems in the allocation of overheads. Buying-in specialist services from another company can also ease relationships but introduces new problems of establishing good contractual relationships.

There is yet another organizational method for trying to make specialists acceptable. Its advocate is, not surprisingly, usually the head of the relevant speciality. This method is to put the head of the department high in the hierarchy, preferably reporting to the managing director. This, it is suggested, will ensure that the speciality will be taken seriously and that its advice and services will be used. A senior position for the manager of the specialist department will bring the advantage of informal contacts, as well as the formal benefits that come from being high up in the hierarchy and participating in top management meetings. The latter is an argument for having the head of information systems both reporting to the chief executive and a member of the top management committee where the subject is of strategic importance to the organization,[6] as it increasingly is in financial institutions, for example. Reporting high up in the organization, though not necessarily to the chief executive in a large company, will help to get the importance of information technology accepted, but it does not assure effective performance for that or for any other specialist activity.

Job rotation between staff and line posts is one method of trying to reduce differences in attitude between the two; the armed services have been doing this for many years. Such job rotation can only occur where the staff job is not a highly professional one that requires long training; for example, there can be no job rotation for lawyers and doctors, though some may spend part of their time in general management and thus learn to appreciate managerial concerns. Specialities which require less training lend themselves to transfer of personnel across departments. Some companies have few career people in personnel, thinking instead that this is a function that should be performed by a manager transferred from an operational department, as part of the training for a top appointment. Such rotation helps to avoid the development of too narrow a specialist outlook. It can also be useful in giving managers some knowledge of the speciality so that they will be in a better position both to use it and to control its practitioners. However, job rotation between operational and specialist departments is no panacea for the problems of relationships between the two. It can help, but with the change of hat an individual's viewpoint tends to change too; misunderstanding and ignorance may be reduced, but there can still be a marked difference in viewpoint.

Project teams, which are set up with a limited life to deal with a particular problem, may be composed of people with both specialist and managerial experience. One by-product of such a team is that members can learn to understand each other's viewpoint. A project team is rarely established for its educational value, but may yet help to improve understanding between its members, while appointments to such a team can contribute to career development.

Finally, here are three tactical guides for the specialist. One is to find out what problem is currently worrying the manager and offer to help. For example, personnel managers who are trying to convince management of the need to take management development seriously may get nowhere if they talk in general terms, but if there is a sudden problem, perhaps of finding a suitable replacement for a particular post, they may be able to point out what needs to be done to avoid such problems in the future. If top management is worried about its ability to attract or to retain good graduates, the specialist may be able to offer a useful analysis of why the company is failing to do so and what needs to be done.

The second tactical guide is to start in an area where success is certain, or almost certain. This is the advice offered by some of the computer consultants. Start with something simple with a sure pay-off, they say; if you start with something that is more ambitious, but which is less certain to succeed, you may have greater success, but if you fail the managers may be disillusioned for a long time. The same tactics are indicated for any new specialist department which is trying to get its service recognized.

The third guide is a negative one. A specialist department that is still struggling to get accepted should try to avoid projects that are likely to raise difficulties for other groups. It may be impossible, or undesirable, to adhere to this guide, but at least the dangers of arousing antagonism should be recognized.

The specialist should always try to involve management in the project whenever it is feasible to do so. Managers will be more interested if they are involved and more likely to continue to use the service or to implement the proposals. Further, they will be able to point out the practical considerations that may be overlooked by the specialist and thus help to ensure that the proposals suit the needs of the department.

SUMMARY

The problems that arise in relations between managers and specialists vary with the organizational relationship. There are four main types of relationship: first, the specialists are on the manager's staff and have no other organizational link; secondly, they are on the manager's staff but are also responsible for their professional competence to the head of their speciality, it is then especially important that the organizational relationship should be clarified; thirdly, they are in a separate department; fourthly, more frequently than before they are outside the organization and employed as consultants. The problems that can exist in these different relationships are discussed. IT and personnel are examples to show how and why the forms of organizational relationship between managers and specialists have changed.

Some types of specialists are much more acceptable than others to managers. McGregor distinguishes between the role of the policeman and that of the professional helper, the latter being more acceptable than the former. The respectability of a speciality also affects its acceptability; advice from old-established professions like medicine or law is not seen as a potential threat to the manager's job, as may advice from newer specialities.

McGregor suggests a number of ways of improving collaboration which still remain true today. His central thesis is that the specialist should act as a professional helper to all levels of management.

Various organizational means are used to facilitate the relationship. One is to put the specialist on the manager's staff. Another is to have specialist departments that provide services only on request and for a fee. Yet another is to put the head of the specialist department high up in the hierarchy. All these methods have snags. Rotation between operational and specialist jobs is used in some organizations as a means of reducing differences in attitudes. Project teams composed of people from both kinds of departments can also help to create understanding between them.

Three tactical guides for the specialist are suggested.

NOTES

1. Herbert Kaufman, *The Forest Ranger: A Study in Administrative Behaviour* (Baltimore, Md: Johns Hopkins University Press, 1960) p. 68.
2. John Dearden, 'The Withering Away of the IS Organization', *Sloan Management Review*, Summer 1987, pp. 87–91.
3. Michael J. Earl, *Management Strategies for Information Technology* (Englewood Cliffs, N. J.: Prentice-Hall, 1987) p. 206.

4. Douglas McGregor, *The Human Side of Enterprise* (New York: McGraw-Hill, 1960) p. 164.
5. Ibid., ch. 12.
6. David Feeny, Brian Edwards and Kep Simpson, *Understanding the CEO/IT Director Relationship* (Oxford: Oxford Institute of Information Management, Templeton College, 1991) Research and Discussion Papers, 91/6.

7 Managerial Relations

Rapid change makes cooperative relations between managers in different departments an essential part of organizational effectiveness. The relations between managers are today more important for organizational effectiveness than in the past. In large organizations there are now many managers who work mainly with other managers. When organizations were smaller and simpler there were few such managers.

The word 'manager' is used very broadly in this chapter to include all those above the level of supervisor, whether or not they have staff reporting to them, such a broad definition being appropriate for a chapter that focuses on peer relations. These relations require the individual to obtain the cooperation of people in other departments. There is a more detailed definition of 'manager' at the start of Chapter 12.

In the past the view of management motivation and behaviour was too simple. The manager tended to be conceived of as an economic man, calculating relative profitabilities and acting accordingly. Research has shown that this conception ignores the other influences upon management behaviour. This chapter describes what research can tell us about managerial relations. It will discuss how managers deal with each other, how their relations can be affected by the situation of the company, what kind of problems arise in these relations and what can be done to try and create organizational loyalty.

A manager is often described as someone who gets things done through other people. We tend to forget that this means that he or she is dependent upon them. The dependence of the manager on other people is one of the key characteristics of the managerial way of life, a characteristic that increases with the complexity of the job. Managers depend upon their superiors for advancement, and often upon colleagues at their own level for help in getting their job done; the relationships with fellow managers are, therefore, vital to the success of their own jobs and future careers.

Managerial relations are changing as a result of changes in the environment of the organization and in technology. In the more stable conditions of the past, clearly marked boundaries separated one department from another. The tasks of each department were well known and relations between departments followed well-established channels. Much of the communications between managers could be written. Oral communications took place mainly vertically, between superior and subordinate, rather than laterally, between members of different departments. In such stable organizations the relations between managers in different departments followed a pattern. The head of each department was the baron of his own domain, subject only to the king, the managing director. Some barons were more important than others, but each knew the boundaries of his own domain and usually respected those of others.

The research of Burns and Stalker first showed how rapid change can affect relations between managers.[1] What has to be done is no longer known; it has to be discovered, and this can most easily be achieved by discussion. Managers must spend much more time talking to each other than is necessary in more stable conditions. The boundaries between departments become less clearly defined. The uncertainty that exists in times of change is likely to lead to difficulties in relations between managers and to provide greater opportunities for playing power politics. Managerial relations, therefore, tend to be more difficult and more important when organizations are experiencing rapid change. This is the state in which almost all organizations find themselves today and almost certainly will continue to do so.

TYPES OF RELATIONS

The distinctive feature about relations between managers in different departments is that they depend upon the individual's capacity to get things done through other people, without the support of formal authority. This can be true even when top management has approved a project. One senior manager who headed a specialist department in a large company presented a proposal to a small committee of the board. They approved. As he left the room one of them said 'Good luck'. It was only later he realized the significance of that remark; even though top management liked his plan, his success would depend upon his ability to enlist the cooperation of other managers.

Sayles made the most illuminating distinction between the different kinds of relations that can exist between managers. He distinguished seven, which he called workflow, trading, service, advisory, auditing, stabilization and innovation.[2] As Sayles says of the first:

> From the manager's point of view, these workflow relationships are crucial. How much he can accomplish depends upon the condition and timing of the 'work' he received from the one or more preceding stages *and* the demands made upon him by those other managers for whose departments his department is the preceding stage.[3]

This kind of dependence is a strain on the relationships between the managers of the departments that are connected by a workflow. There is a tendency to blame others for delays which make the work of one's own department more difficult. The department that comes earlier in the workflow can also be a convenient scapegoat to excuse one's own failings. The character of these relationships depends upon the personalities concerned, their feelings for each other and their concern for organizational, as distinct from narrowly departmental, objectives. These relationships can be eased by recognizing their existence and, where feasible, by formalizing them; that is, by specifying the responsibilities for each part of the workflow and the procedures to be followed. The importance of these workflow relations should, therefore, be recognized in the relevant job descriptions, but this is rarely done except in the most general terms. There is a need, too, to ensure that managers in a workflow relationship keep in touch with each other. This is essential when they are working on something new, otherwise there is a danger that the work of one section may conflict with the work of another in its content or timing.

Another type of relationship that Sayles discusses is the trading one. He calls this 'the process by which the terms of some future relationship are established'.[4] One trading relationship is that between service departments and their customers; another is that between the manager who is responsible for completing a task and the other individuals and groups in the organization whose help is needed to do so. Sayles thinks that, although these trading relations within organizations are similar to those between buyers and sellers outside them, there are some differences. The constraints upon the buyer may be somewhat greater than in the market-place, where one can negotiate with other salesmen. There may also be a multi-price system: 'Good friends (or those offering more interesting or desirable projects) may get lower prices than organizational enemies or those requesting less pleasant services.' Sayles bases this latter statement on a study he did of contracting-out versus in-plant maintenance, where great variability in the addition of overheads to various cost estimates was observed.[5]

Sayles sees trading relationships as a crucial aspect of many managers' jobs. He thinks that some managers resent this type of relationship and want instead rules to decide who does what, with whom and on what terms. He suggests that this kind of relationship will become more important as the boundaries of organizations become more fluid. Increasingly, managers have trading relationships both inside and outside the organization, as a wider variety of work is contracted out.

The price that is paid in a trading relationship between two members of the same organization is not necessarily a monetary one. A service department may sell its services, but often the price is some reciprocal aid. There may be an explicit agreement – 'I will help you, if you will do so and so', although it may also be implicit, for example the recognition of an obligation which can be drawn on in the future.

Sayles's discussion of trading relationships is concerned with manufacturing industry, but one can notice similar relationships in diverse types of organization. Blau and Scott describe reciprocal consultation in a social service agency.[6] Where the consultation is only in one direction, the price paid is the acknowledgement that one's colleague is more expert than oneself. Those who do not want to acknowledge an inferior status take care not to ask one person too often for advice. Similar reactions can be found in universities, where the help that is given to a colleague either creates a reciprocal obligation, such as to help later with a student or to read the draft of a book, or the acceptance of a difference in informal status.

The studies by Sayles and by Blau and Scott were done in the mid-1960s. They were new contributions then that showed the reality of one aspect of managerial work, but such trading relationships remain a feature of managers' jobs today in all kinds of organizations. Indeed, in times of rapid change they become more important. This is true in British and American organizations, particularly for junior- and middle-management jobs. American management literature, especially, has a great deal about the importance of such relationships and about the need for establishing reciprocal relationships with managers inside and outside the organization – 'networking' is the word used. However, we should not think of management only from the Anglo-American perspective. In Germany, for example, relations between managers are different. There is less alliance building across boundaries and relations are more formal.[7]

A study by Trought of the lateral contacts made during one week by 21 managers in manufacturing management in five companies provides unusually detailed information about the nature of these contacts.[8] The contacts were brief and mainly face-to-face; of the 373 lateral contacts made by the 21 managers 71 per cent were face-to-face, with a median time of 3 minutes, and 29 per cent were on the telephone, with a median time of 2 minutes. This finding is similar to those of studies of all contacts. Trought also studied the nature of the relationship and comments:

Conflict, as a feature of organizational sociology, seems to have been overstudied. My data suggests that human cooperation more accurately reflects a large proportion of industrial relationships, particularly in the lateral dimension, than does conflict.[9]

He recorded 117 cooperative contacts, compared with five conflicting ones, all these contacts being within manufacturing management. Conflicts may be more likely between different functions in a company, though we do not have a comparative study to prove this; evidence about interdepartmental battles is merely anecdotal.

Jane Hannaway has highlighted other aspects of managerial behaviour and of relations between managers. She studied 52 American school administrators at three management levels, in the central office of a school district, and related her findings to those of previous researchers. She points out that much managerial interaction is about the acquisition and clarification of information. Since much information that managers work with is soft data, part of their time is spent scanning for information. She comments that a good deal of managerial information seems to be acquired by an

> almost random scanning process, in which neither the payoff nor even the object of the search is well defined. Walking down a hall, for example, I often heard one manager casually say to another, 'How did the meeting go this morning'. Sometimes the response was simply, 'Fine'. But more often a conversation ensued in which one manager described what was interesting or important about the meeting and then this was interpreted – maybe as a potential problem that should be monitered or perhaps simply as a lead-in to another topic – by the second manager. A good part of a manager's day is spent this way.[10]

She concludes:

> In the dynamic environment in which most managers work, there are no natural limits to information acquisition. Events must be constantly defined and interpreted and then redefined and reinterpreted.[11]

She suggests that 'groping' may be a realistic way to describe part of managerial behaviour.

Another aspect of managerial behaviour that she highlights is that of 'signalling'. She points out that in the school district she studied it was hard to judge good performance – this uncertainty about the relation between managerial actions and outcomes is true of much public-sector work – so that part of the time of the managers she studied was spent in signalling their worth to other people. Managers, she argues, are interested in their own welfare as well as in that of the organization, so such signalling is a way to forward their own career interests.[12]

DIFFERENCES BETWEEN MANAGERIAL JOBS

The difficulties that arise in interdepartmental relations are partly due to conflicts between the aims of individual departments. They are also due to differences in the nature of the jobs and in the personal attributes that these jobs require. An American study looked at difference between the attributes of managers in four functions: engineering and research and development; sales; administration and accounting; and production.[13] Two hundred and fifty managers in more than a dozen companies were given intelligence and personality tests and interviews. The main difference between managers in the four functions were found to be in intelligence, education and professional knowledge, although there were also some personality differences. Commenting on the effects of one of these differences on interdepartmental relations, the researchers said:

> These findings suggest that, in most companies, the sales group will be the most assertive and the most vocal, and that in promoting this function, its members may tend to take a narrow and somewhat selfish point of view. Such a tendency can be dangerous for the company as a whole and should, therefore, be controlled. Top management should also recognize the dangers of the sales group's tendency to impetuosity . . . Because of their verbal ability and aggressiveness, sales executives may be able to disclaim responsibility for their errors and project them on other groups in the company.

There is no comparable recent study but personality tests that can be used for vocational guidance, such as the Myers Briggs, show the personality differences of different occupational groups.

The author's study of how 160 managers spent their time for four weeks found that the sample could be divided into five groups, distinguished by their different working patterns. The most distinctive group was the one that was mainly composed of production managers. Their working days were more fragmented than those of the other groups of managers. They spent more time with their subordinates than other groups and less time with people outside the department.[14] In contrast the working environment of the sales manager is very different. The sales department is under pressure both from the works and from the customers. Salesmen may feel personally involved in relationships with their customers, although this will vary somewhat with the kind of company, as well as with the individual. They will hate to say 'No' to a customer. They may try and get special treatment for particular customers, without considering whether it pays the organization to do so or not. In these ways, they are likely to think differently from those in production. Nowadays it is more common for managers to get experience in other departments, so that the functional differences may be less strong, but they still remain.

There are just as great contrasts to be found in other types of organizations. In local government the treasurer comes from a different professional background to the education officer or the social services officer; the pattern of their working day and the people they are in contact with will also differ. Such jobs are likely to attract different kinds of people, and these differences are further strengthened by training. The contrasts between the working experience of managers in different occupations and departments intensify the problems of communication between them.

We are generally more conscious of barriers to communications between different levels in the hierarchy than of those between departments. However, the latter can be as equally important as the former, especially in times of change, when more interdepartmental communications are necessary. At such times it needs to be made easy for people to talk to each other, so that they are not inhibited from asking others for information and advice. Burns and Stalker described well what is wanted:

> The operation of an organic system of management hinges on effective communication. This is much more than a matter of providing, through the distribution of paper, for notification of events and decisions affecting functionally related persons and departments. It is also something more than providing for exchanges of information and opinion in meetings. What is essential is that nothing should inhibit individuals from applying to others for information and advice, or for additional effort. This in turn depends on the ability to suppress differences of status and of technical prestige on occasions of working interaction, and on the absence of barriers to communication founded on functional preserves, privilege, or personal reserve.[15]

The establishment of quality circles has been one of the more recent methods used to try and ease communication between levels, particularly between the shop floor and management.

The growing use of Email for the exchange of information provides a new means of reducing barriers to communication caused by hierarchical differences. However, this is most likely to be useful for relatively hard information in a technical environment. It is unlikely to reduce the problem of barriers to communication for soft information and in less technically based organizations.

THE POWER STRUCTURE

The dominant factor in managerial relations, particularly at the level of top management, is the existence of a power structure. This fact is rarely openly acknowledged. Many managers talk of decision-making as if it was a wholly rational choice between alternatives, based on the assessment of the profitability of different courses of action in a business, and on their contribution to furthering the objectives of the organization. Any observer of the process of decision-making will notice that, though arguments are likely to be couched in rational terms, the relative weight that is given to different arguments, and the kind of arguments that are put forward, may well be determined by the policies of the different political factions. The decision that is reached may depend on the relative strength of these factions. Few questions are so clearcut that there is obviously only one rational decision. Some decisions, of course, do not affect the power structure, but even then different political factions may develop; for example, the decision as to which make of computer to buy should not, at first sight, have any effect on the balance of power between departments, or between individuals, yet it can become the source of a political battle between supporters and opponents of different makes.

The power structure can affect the type of decision that is reached. It also commonly delays it. The more the decision is likely to affect the balance of power, the longer the delay is likely to be. In government we talk about the need to reach a politically acceptable decision and the time that it may take to do so. A politically acceptable decision may mean one that is generally acceptable, or one that is acceptable to the supporters of the party in power. Whichever it is, there are limits to what the government can do. Here the sanction against infringing these limits is that the voters will reject the party that does so. Equally, there are also sanctions in business and other organizations; for example, senior managers may resign or their enthusiasm and cooperation may decline. Hence most managements will delay if they can reaching a decision that causes strong opposition, in the hope that opinions may change or a more acceptable pretext for the need to take the decision may turn up.

Chief executives of organizations should be sensitive to the political line-up amongst the senior managers, otherwise they may make a decision that upsets the power structure too much. The results of one such decision reached by a chief executive when confronted with a disagreement between several of the senior managers was, as one of those present put it, like 'the breaking of a very valuable Chinese vase. Everyone stood around horrified and no one had the resilience to try and pick up the pieces again.'

Power battles are more common at senior management levels than they are lower down. One explanation is that senior managers who head large departments or divisions have more at stake. Another is that relations are much more personal in a small top management group. Yet another explanation is that it is the more politically conscious and ambitious people who reach top management. Whatever the reasons, the atmosphere there, particularly in a large organization, is likely to be different from that lower down. As one junior manager who had to attend senior management meetings said: 'When I tell my contemporaries how senior managers behave, they don't believe me, but then they have not watched these power battles.'

The prevalence of power politics has important implications for those who want to get new ideas accepted. It is common for young specialists and managers, particularly if they are scientifically trained, to believe that logical arguments alone are sufficient to get a proposal accepted. They may be insensitive to the ways in which people react to their proposals and to the importance of trying to persuade them that their ideas are good ones. They may be unaware of the need to discover who are the most powerful people in the organization – not necessarily conveyed by looking at an organization chart – and to make a special effort to convince them of the value of their proposals, or at least to try and ensure that they do not antagonize them.

The implications of the prevalence of power politics are important for top management too. The chief executive and other top managers create conditions that encourage or discourage power politics. When there are issues that affect the interests of powerful individuals or groups, the discussion should be aimed at trying to resolve the problem rather than at creating a win-or-lose situation. Here the example set by top management, and especially by the chief executive or by the chairman of a committee discussing the issue, can help to set the tone of the discussion.

Top management can also set the climate within which competition for promotion will be conducted. Organizations vary widely in the ways in which this competition is conducted. Public organizations seek to depersonalize promotion and to make it as objective as possible. Companies usually have a much less formalized, more secretive approach to deciding who shall be promoted. However, with the advent of assessment centres this is less true than it used to be. In all organizations, promotion is likely to be a subject for power politics. The more senior the appointment, the more of it there is likely to be. The harder it is to make objective judgements of performance the more ambitious managers will take to signalling the importance of their contributions. The politics surrounding promotion is a fact that those responsible for making the appointment should recognize and should try to avoid exacerbating. It is also a fact that those ambitious for promotion should remember.

Differences in power between managers at the same level in the hierarchy is a fact of organizational life. It should not be deplored: it is how it is exercised and the reasons why it exists that matter. Salancik and Pfeffer, who studied power in universities, insurance companies and hospitals in the US, argue that it can be the secret of organizational success because those who cope best with the critical problems of the organization acquire power.[16]

CREATING LOYALTY TO ORGANIZATIONAL GOALS

One of the reasons for power politics is that individuals and departments identify with their own goals rather than with those of the organization as a whole. Divisions and departments are likely to develop their own aims, which may conflict with each other as well as with the company's aim of maximizing profitability. The problem, therefore, is how to get managers to subordinate their individual and local aims to the aims of the organization as a whole. The larger the organization the greater the problem of doing so is likely to be.

Japanese companies appear to have solved the problem of obtaining the commitment of their employees. How do they do this? Students of Japanese management have tried to answer this question as part of the search for the secrets of Japanese competitive success in international markets. One of the American writers about Japanese management, William Ouchi, has said that there are American counterparts of the Japanese management system. He calls their approach Theory Z,[17] and maintains that it consists of a mixture of strategies and techniques to build organizational loyalty.[18]

The three strategies of Theory Z are long-term employment, a unique organizational philosophy which gives a clear statement of objectives and values, and intensive socialization of recruits who are carefully selected. These strategies are supported by six management techniques:

1. Job rotation and slow promotions. A policy of lifetime employment means that promotion must be slow unless the organization is expanding rapidly, so mobility is achieved mainly by lateral transfers. Such transfers develop staff who are generalists rather than specialists.
2. Complex appraisal system which emphasizes a variety of personal characteristics and group as well as individual performance. These

appraisals take account of the longer term and so make it safer for managers to take calculated risks. There is not the same stress as in many American companies upon achievement of short-term results.

3. Emphasis on work groups, that is assigning tasks for groups and leaving the group members to decide the best way of carrying them out.

4. Open communication encouraged by the contacts developed through job rotation and the heavy emphasis on groups.

5. Consultative decision-making based on informal discussion and consultation with all who may be affected.

6. Concern for the employee. Managers spend much of their time talking to employees about everyday matters. Senior managers regularly talk with workers so as to learn about their concerns. An important part of a manager's appraisal is a measure of the quality of their relations with subordinates.

American companies which adopt many aspects of this approach include IBM, Procter & Gamble and Hewlett–Packard. British companies in the car industry have been adopting many of these strategies in their search for ways of competing more effectively with Japanese car makers.

Theory Z is about how to obtain organizational loyalty amongst employees generally. However, there can also be the problem of getting such commitment amongst a top management group, where the danger is of rivalry and lack of cooperation. An early study by Katz gives an unusually good description, which is still relevant today, of how organizational loyalty was achieved amongst the top management of an American company.[19] He studied the behaviour of the president (managing director) and the six senior executives of a medium-size American company in a consumer-goods industry. Each of the senior executives either headed a function, such as production or sales, or a product division. Katz said that collaboration amongst this top-management group was facilitated by the following factors:

1. *A well-defined social structure* which came from the long experience that six of the seven executives had in working together in their present positions. Their relative statuses and roles had become established, as had their codes of behaviour.

2. *Shared values.* Katz gives a number of examples, among them the fact that five of the executives were primarily sales-orientated.

3. *Acknowledgement of technical expertise.* Each of the seven was recognized as the technical expert on particular problems.

4. *Free interchange*, encouraged by little stress on titles or job descriptions, consultations with people at any level who had relevant expertise, and a physical layout with few partitions or walls.
5. *Identification with the company* because each of the top executives thought that his reputation depended upon the success of the company as a whole.
6. *Penalties for deviant behaviour* by, for example, withdrawing support from anyone who did not observe the norms described above, such as free interchange.
7. *Organizational structure built around individuals.* 'Each man performed those duties in which he was perceived as having greater ability than anyone else in the organization, in which he had interest, and in which he felt most comfortable. Advancement depended largely on ability to understand and utilize the system of informal interchange, and to establish one's own acknowledged area of competence.'
8. *A team with all necessary skills.* 'In the top-management group, there existed adequate technical skill to cope with the company's most important recurring problems, sufficient human relations skill to maintain a high degree of personal respect, and a well-defined "conceptual skill" (in the president) for visualizing the relationships of the various aspects to one another.'

The role of the president as the prime coordinator was well established, but it led to domination by the president and dependency on the part of the senior executives.

Other companies may use other methods, there being no single set of answers to the problem of how to create a cohesive management group. Shared beliefs – that is, a common management philosophy – are important. This is a consideration that is sometimes taken into account by managements when discussing a possible merger. It can be disruptive to attempt to merge with a company whose managers have a different philosophy about, for example, the way to treat employees. Participation in the formation of objectives is another, and complementary, way of trying to achieve identification with common objectives.

Managers in different departments and in different occupations will, as we have seen, have dissimilar job experiences and may have different personality characteristics. To offset these differences there need to be opportunities for shared experiences and for the development of common beliefs. In a small organization, departmental managers will be in close contact with each other but in large organizations they can be quite isolated. Common experience can be provided by interdepartmental job transfer, by internal training courses, and by other opportunities for managers to get together. Managers' dining-rooms are one means of doing this, though they have the drawback of stressing the difference between managers and their subordinates. Interdepartmental meetings, unless they become power battlegrounds, are another way of bridging across departments. 'Away days' have become much more common as top managers seek to involve their staff in the discussion of new policies and in plans for their successful implementation.

Corporate loyalty has its dangers as well as its advantages. Managers may identify too much with the organization so that they lose the capacity for looking critically at it. They may produce too few new ideas themselves and be unreceptive to new ideas from outside. This can lead to stagnation. It is a danger that large organizations, especially those which aim to do much of their recruiting direct from schools and universities, need to guard against. Hence the origins of a new phrase since the late 1980s, 'organizational learning', which is discussed in Chapter 12.

SUMMARY

The nature of the relations that exist between managers is an important factor in determining how the organization works. The chapter describes what research can tell us about these relations. Managers are dependent both upon other managers for the success of their work, and upon their boss and their subordinates. The importance of relations between colleagues increases in times of rapid change, when much more lateral communication is necessary.

There are many different types of relations between managers. Sayles describes seven. Two are discussed in this chapter – the workflow and trading relations. Both can be crucial for the success of a manager's own work.

Relations between managers are made more complicated by the fact that they often work in very different types of jobs. These jobs tend to attract different personalities and these differences are accentuated by training and experience.

Effective relations between managers depend upon good communications. This is most important in times of change, when it is essential that people should be able to talk freely to each other without feeling inhibited in asking for information and advice.

Power politics are a characteristic of organizational life: this fact can affect the nature of decisions that are made and the time it takes to make them. A sensitivity to the power politics of an organization can be important for those who want promotion, for the would-be innovator and for top management. The latter can seek to shift the emphasis in a discussion from win-or-lose to a problem-solving approach. The chief executive sets the code of conduct within which managerial relations take place.

All organizations need to try and create a corporate loyalty so that managers identify with the organization's goals, and not with their own narrow individual or departmental goals. The strategies and techniques used by Japanese companies and some Japanese-style American companies show one way of creating this loyalty. The development of shared beliefs will contribute to managerial cohesion but it should not be forgotten that this can also have its dangers: love can be blind.

NOTES

1. T. Burns and G. M. Stalker, *The Management of Innovation*, 2nd edn (London: Tavistock, 1966).
2. Leonard R. Sayles, *Managerial Behaviour: Administration in Complex Organizations* (New York: McGraw-Hill, 1964) pp. 49–51.
3. Ibid., p. 68.
4. Ibid., p. 60.
5. Ibid., p. 62.
6. Peter M. Blau and Richard W. Scott, *Formal Organizations: A Comparative Approach* (London: Routledge & Kegan Paul, 1963; paperback edn, 1966) pp. 128–39.
7. John Mole, *Mind Your Manners* (London: Industrial Society, 1990) p. 42.
8. Brian Trought, *An Analysis of Lateral Relations in Manufacturing Management*, doctoral thesis, University of Nottingham, 1984.
9. Ibid., p. 213.
10. Jane Hannaway, *Managers Managing: The Workings of an Administrative System* (London: Oxford University Press, 1989) p. 63.
11. Ibid.
12. Ibid., p. 143.
13. L. Hutter, S. Levy, E. Rosen and M. Stopal, 'Further Light on the Executive Personality', *Personnel*, vol. 36, no. 2 (Mar.–Apr. 1959) pp. 42–50.
14. Rosemary Stewart, *Managers and Their Jobs*, 2nd edn (London: Macmillan, 1988) ch. 6.
15. Burns and Stalker, *Management of Innovation*, p. 252.
16. Gerald R. Salancik and Jeffrey Pfeffer, 'Who Gets Power – and How They Hold on to It: A Strategic-Contingency Model of Power', *Organizational Dynamics*, Special Reports (New York: American Management Association, 1988) pp. 3–21.
17. William G. Ouchi, *Theory Z: How American Business Can Meet the Japanese Challenge* (New York: Addison-Wesley, 1981).

18.   A summary of, and commentary upon, Theory Z is given by Stephen P. Robbins, 'The Theory Z Organization from a Power-Control Perspective', *California Management Review*, vol. XXV, no. 2 (January 1983) pp. 67–75.
19.   Extracts from unpublished doctoral dissertation, Harvard Business School, 1956; Robert L. Katz, 'Executive Teamwork: Top Management Coordination in a Medium-sized Company', in Paul R. Lawrence, *Organizational Behavior and Administration: Cases, Concepts, and Research Findings*, rev. edn (Reading, Mass.: Richard D. Irwin and Dorsey Press, rev. edn, 1965) pp. 602–4.

8 How Much Decentralization?

Two of the most important decisions to be made in any organization are 'How decentralized should the organization be?' and 'What decisions should be delegated?'[1] These are the questions discussed in this chapter. The first question is about general policy, the second asks about the way in which it should be implemented.

The heads of very small businesses do not have to decide what decisions they should delegate, since they can make them all themselves. They may continue to try and do so as their business grows, but their future success will depend, in part, both on their willingness to delegate and on their ability to decide correctly what decisions they should delegate and which ones they should take themselves.

Bosses who do not delegate sufficiently – that is, who do not give subordinates authority to act – will find that even though they appoint extra staff to ease their load, subordinates are always coming to them for decisions. They will have no opportunity to think, at least while they are at work, about the main problems of the business, as they will be always being asked about details. They may become like the managing director of a medium-sized family firm who had to see visitors in the waiting-room because his office was full of papers awaiting his attention and besieged by staff wanting decisions. In larger organizations today this is likely to be less of a problem than in the past. In slimmed-down organizations managers have more people reporting to them; they have to learn to delegate if they are to be able to cope with their greater and wider-ranging responsibilities.

WHAT IS DECENTRALIZATION?

All organizations can be pictured as somewhere on a continuum, with centralization at one end and decentralization at the other. At no point can one draw a line and say that those on one side are centralized and those on the other are not. One can only talk about organization as being more or less centralized or decentralized. Even then there are difficulties. How do you compare the extent of centralization in different organizations? There was

103

much more interest in doing so in the 1960s and 1970s, when more importance was attached to the nature of the formal organization, than there is today. Examples of this past interest are an American Management Association's questionnaire survey in the mid-1960s, which asked questions like 'Who makes the final decisions for the company as a whole, or for a particular division of it, on such matters as pricing policy, salaries over a certain level and the creation of new departments?' 'Are there definite limits set on expenditure?' 'If so, what amount of money requires the approval of the board?'[2]

Pugh and his colleagues in the 1960s devoted a lot of research effort to developing indices for comparing different types of organizations. One of their indices is of centralization. They developed a standard list of 37 recurrent decisions and asked: 'Who is the last person whose assent must be obtained before legitimate action is taken, even if others have subsequently to confirm the decision?' Organizations were scored from 0 to 5 for each decision, according to the level at which the decision was taken. The total score on the 37 items was the measure of the amount of centralization.[3] This measure, or adaptations of it, was used in many later studies. It has been criticized as misleadingly precise because it ignores the possibility of influence; a superior may take a decision on the advice of subordinates, for example. These critics have sought to assess the amount of centralization by asking *how* decisions are taken rather than *where* they are taken.

The use of factual measures to assess the amount of centralization or decentralization has its limitations, as Kaufman pointed out in his study of the US Forest Service:

> If experimentation discloses that field behaviour can be controlled as effectively by inculcating the fact and value premises of central headquarters upon the minds of field men *without* extensive use of close supervisory and enforcement procedures, as is possible *with* these devices, then an organization which gives every indication of decentralization by all the usual indices may in fact be as fully governed from the centre as one without these visible paraphernalia of central direction . . . The usual criteria stress external forms and tend to neglect actual behaviour.[4]

Perrow, writing 14 years later, also pointed out the dangers.

> We should not measure decentralization by the level at which people may hire, fire or spend a few thousand dollars without proper authorization, we must also measure the unobtrusive controls.[5]

Kaufman was one of the early voices of protest against thinking of the reality of organizational life too much in terms of formal structure. Over 30 years later the importance of organizational culture in influencing what people do, which is what Kaufman described, is all the vogue. Yet the extent of decentralization, and what should be decentralized, are still important decisions within organizations and so is delegation for the individual manager.

HOW MUCH DECENTRALIZATION?

Using decentralization in the sense of greater decision-making authority at the lower levels in the hierarchy, there is no easy answer to the question 'How much decentralization should there be?' The answer may well vary with the type of organization, the stage in its development and between different parts of the organization. The size of the organization is obviously important; the larger it is, the stronger the arguments for decentralization, because of the problems of effectively controlling a large organization from the centre and at the same time giving junior and middle managers some scope for initiative. There are other factors that must be considered too. One of these is the diversity of activities and the extent to which top management can adequately understand them. It is easier to centralize effectively a large company which is engaged in one main activity, such as steel-making, than a company which is engaged in a variety of dissimilar activities. The rate of change may also limit the amount of centralization that is possible; where operating conditions are changing rapidly, more may have to be left to the judgement of the person on the spot. Moreover, rapidly changing technology may enforce delegation of some decisions because it is likely to be the junior staff who are most technically up to date and who understand the latest developments.

The amount of decentralization that top management thinks is desirable will depend on how far it wants common policies. If it favours common policies in the main areas of the business it can still decentralize, provided that there are well-established procedures and a common management outlook to give top management some assurance that the organization will continue to be managed in a consistent way. It is more difficult to achieve this combination of objectives in a newly created organization that is composed of many undertakings which were previously separate. Public organizations that are expected to have consistent policies in the treatment of their clients or employees must be more centralized than organizations which are not under such an obligation. However, the need for centralization can be at least partly offset by the establishment of rules and procedures.

The calibre of staff at all levels will also affect the amount of decentralization that is possible. Decentralization presupposes staff who are competent
to take decisions, both in terms of their ability and their knowledge. Developing countries are usually short of skilled workers and experienced clerical
and managerial staff, so that there may be few suitable people to delegate to.
Companies opening up subsidiaries in such countries may find that they
have to rethink what kind of decisions should be taken at different levels.
Yet another factor that can limit delegation is the burden of work already
born by subordinates. As one general manager in the NHS said: 'Yes, I
know that I ought to delegate more, but when I look at my staff I see that
they already have so much to do that they are likely to crack if I try to shed
any of my own load.'

The answer that top management gives to the question 'How much
decentralization?' will also depend upon its philosophy. Does top management believe that their juniors must learn by being given the freedom to
make mistakes? Does it think that people work harder if they are given
plenty of scope for initiative, or does it believe that people tend to be lazy
and need to be directed and controlled to ensure that they do what is
wanted? Does top management believe that it necessarily knows best, that
there is no substitute for the years of experience that it has had? The kind of
answers that management gives to such questions will determine whether it
favours a policy of centralization or one of decentralization.

BALANCING ADVANTAGES AND DISADVANTAGES

Unfortunately for the organization planner – and that term should include,
at least to some extent, every manager – both centralization and decentralization have advantages and disadvantages. The aim should therefore be to
try and find out what is the most appropriate balance between the two
extremes for a particular organization in the circumstances that operate at a
particular time. The advantages of centralization are the disadvantages of
decentralization and vice versa, so that we need only consider the advantages and disadvantages of one of them.

Let us look at decentralization. The advantages of decentralization are as
follows:

1. It encourages initiative.
2. It makes junior and middle management jobs more interesting.
3. 1 and 2 make it easier to recruit good managers and retain them.

4. It is easier to judge managers' performances if they are made responsible for a decentralized unit of the organization.
5. Decisions are more likely to be taken by those who will have to live with their results.
6. Decisions made closer to the actual situations are likely to be more realistic.
7. Decisions are likely to be made more quickly.

The concomitant disadvantages of decentralization are:

1. It is harder for top management to exercise control over what people are doing, or even to know what decisions they are taking.
2. There is a danger that the perspective of managers of decentralized units may be too limited. They may think too much in terms of local advantages and not enough about the good of the organization as a whole.
3. Administrative costs are likely to be greater because decentralized units will probably have their own specialists.

Management's view as to what is the most suitable balance between centralization and decentralization often changes over time. There is unlikely to be a stable equilibrium between the advantages and disadvantages of the chosen policy. A policy of greater decentralization, for example, is likely to have continuing and, perhaps, snowballing effects. Top management may feel that the managers lower down have taken too much initiative or are too much out of their control. Alternatively, if top management has been following a policy of centralization of many decisions, it may find that it is losing some of its brighter young men and women, or that managers lower down are not taking initiative even when top management expect them to.

There are pessimists who believe that you are more likely to get the advantages of centralization or decentralization in the early stages of a change to one policy or the other, and that the disadvantages will gradually become more evident, so that another change eventually becomes desirable. This may explain why large organizations often change their policy in different directions. As one top manager put it,'You begin to think you ought to change because you become more conscious of the failings of your present policy and persuade yourself that a change must surely be an improvement.'

The extensive research into decentralization provides no clear guidelines for the manager because many of the findings are contradictory.[6] We cannot simply recommend more or less decentralization, because the decision depends on so many different factors. Decentralization cannot be considered by itself.

There is a danger of thinking that decentralization is the general response today to the problems faced by companies in a rapidly changing world. However, a study by Hilary Ingram in the second part of 1989 of organizational changes in 87 companies in the UK insurance industry found the reverse. Many of these companies had decentralized by setting up separate divisions for different aspects of their business, but at the time of the survey the dominant trend was to recentralization mainly because of poor performance, though another reason for some was a new acquisition.[7] This unexpected finding of recentralization may be an illustration of the tendency of managements to become disillusioned with their current form of organization and to believe that a change will be an improvement.

CRITERIA FOR DELEGATION

We have talked about decentralization in general as a policy that management may choose to adopt. Once such a policy decision is made there comes the difficult problem of deciding what should be delegated and to whom, or, in a large organization, to what level in the hierarchy. Today, where the presumption in many organizations is for decentralization, the question is more likely to be put the other way round: 'What decisions do top management need to take themselves?'

Top management needs to decide what decisions matter most to the success of the organization. The answer will vary from industry to industry: in pharmaceuticals research and development decisions are the most vital to the success of the company; in many consumer-goods industries, marketing decisions are the most important; in the oil industry, assessment of international political risks is a major consideration for top management – efficient production and good marketing policies are of little avail if supplies of oil are cut off and no adequate alternatives developed. In all organizations a supply of good managers will be important for their future success. In the British Civil Service one of the guides to the importance of a decision is whether or not it is in a politically sensitive area, that is whether a decision will lead to a question in the House of Commons. In large diverse companies long-range strategy, major investments and the appointment of senior managers are the subjects most commonly reserved for top management.

The relative importance of a decision, judged by its effect on the organization's objectives, is one guide as to who should take it. Of course there are other criteria, of which the most important are:

1. What information is necessary to take the decision? Who has this information?
2. What knowledge is necessary to take the decision? Who has this knowledge?
3. How easily can the information be transferred to those with the necessary knowledge?
4. What are the likely consequences of taking a wrong decision? How important is it that the best decision should be taken?
5. How urgent is the decision? What are the consequences of a delay in taking it?

The relative importance of these different guides will depend both upon the characteristics of the organization and upon management's policies. In selling and in buying, the ability to take a rapid decision may sometimes make the difference between a deal and no deal. In companies where this is the case, decisions may have to be delegated to the person on the spot, subject perhaps to a telephone query to the boss. Equally, speed may be vital in saving the life of an injured person so there may not be time to wait for a professional opinion. Yet even here the importance attached to speed will depend upon the environment. In the United States, doctors are reluctant to stop to attend to people injured in motor accidents because of the danger that the patient or a relative may sue the doctor for inadequate treatment.

Banks differ in the importance they attach to a speedy decision when a customer asks for a loan. The management of a bank which has a policy of letting customers know quickly whether they can have a loan is more likely to delegate this authority than a bank where the management has different priorities.

Some decisions need two kinds of knowledge: that which comes from having the feel of the local situation; and that which comes from knowing where the local situation fits into the wider picture. The person on the spot may understand the local situation better than a more experienced, more highly trained manager who is in a distant office, but the latter is in a better position to judge the possible effect of a local decision on other parts of the organization. Hence the need to decide what decisions need this wider perspective; this may have nothing to do with ability but merely reflect the type of job and the location. This was strikingly shown by one manager who was standing in for her chief at a divisional office. While she was there she disallowed some of the requests that she had made in her normal job. Asked why she had done so, she replied that 'it looks different from here'. The works manager is likely to understand the shop steward, better than the industrial relations specialist at head office, but the latter is more likely to be able to assess the possible repercussions of a decision in one plant on shop stewards in other parts of the company.

We have talked as though management always made a conscious choice about where decisions should be taken. However, decisions are not always the result of a deliberate choice. They can emerge without anybody being certain who has taken the decision, when it was taken, or even being aware that a decision was made.

Management should consider what kind of decisions should be taken at different levels in the organization, but it should also remember that what is decided in theory may well be different from what happens in practice. On the one hand, people may be frightened to accept responsibility for decisions and so push them back up the line. On the other hand, some individuals may take decisions that should have been referred to their boss. Management needs to check from time to time to see where decisions are actually being taken, or whether they are being taken at all.

One advantage that some companies have obtained from systems analysis is a knowledge of where some decisions actually are made. This can be a shock, as in one large company where it emerged that vital decisions were being taken by a clerk and were not being reviewed.

There are those who used to argue that managements only decentralized because they had to, because they could not cope with information required for centralized decision-making. If it became easier for them to cope, then they would want to have more centralization. This was the argument of writers who predicted that computers would lead to greater centralization, as they can provide top management with more and better information.[8] So far there is no clear evidence that this is happening. The computer may reduce the number of decisions that *must* be decentralized because the information can now be made quickly available for senior management, but it will not affect the judgement of what decisions should be decentralized, except where the computer makes it clearly more economic to centralize decision-making. One example where this is true is the utilization of cash balances in different parts of the organization. Since interest can be earned overnight, central information about cash balances can be used to increase the income received. Otherwise top management's decision on what should be centralized will be made in part from its judgement of what are the key areas of the business to which it ought to be attending.

FEDERALISM OR DECENTRALIZATION?

Some writers now argue that federalism is the way that companies should be organized in the modern world and that the concept of decentralization conveys the wrong idea.[9] The difference between the two is that in decentralization the centre delegates some of its power to its divisions, whereas in federalism the divisions give some of their power to the centre for the good of all. The idea comes from the origins of the USA with the individual states ceding some of their power to the federal government. The EC is a contemporary analogy.

The advantages of the federal analogy is that it conveys a different picture from the traditional one of a powerful head office as a necessary part of any large organization. The limits to the successful use of central power was the reason for the original interest in decentralization. The much more rapid rate of change affecting organizations made decentralization even more necessary. The idea of a federal organization goes even further. Two of its protagonists, James O'Toole and Warren Bennis, suggest that the ideal federation is non-centralized rather than decentralized; that is, power is withheld from the centre by its constituent parts.[10] Again the EC is an example.

How useful is the idea of 'federalism' as a contribution to thinking about the basic organizational problems of where decisions are to be taken and of who is exercising control and by what means? It is useful in helping people to think more flexibly about these basic problems, but probably not more than that. Christopher Lorenz, writing in the *Financial Times*, rightly pointed out the limitations to the federal analogy applied to business, where it is top management who decide how much power to give to the divisions and who usually retain the power to make their top appointments.[11]

CONTROL

One of top management's concerns about the decentralization is that it may not be able to exercise sufficient control over what is being done. This fear may stem from too narrow a view of the ways in which control can be exercised. It should be clear from the earlier references to control by influencing the way that people think that centralized control is not the only option. Child usefully summarizes and discusses the options that are available.[12] The first he calls *personal centralized control*, often found in small owner-controlled businesses; it is centralized decision-making supported by personal inspection and leadership. The second is *bureaucratic control*, which is control by formal procedures, rules and task definition; it is discussed in the next chapter, 'Order versus Flexibility'. The third he calls *output control*. This is one of the controls that can be exercised in a decentralized organization, and includes the setting of annual targets. The time for agreeing targets is a tense period of the year in any company where the assessment of performance against targets is rigorously applied. Managements that use output controls need to design jobs and units so that their performance can be measured, and rewards and penalties can then be linked to achieving the performance specified. The fourth form of control is *cultural*. It is illustrated in the quotation from Kaufman earlier in this chapter and in much current discussion about the importance of culture and about the strategies and techniques of Japanese management. The emphasis in cultural control is on selection, training and intensive socialization in the customary ways of thinking and acting in the organization.

The first form of control is only possible in smaller organizations. The other methods of control are likely to be used to some extent in most organizations. It is the relative emphasis on each that distinguishes between them. Where the third and fourth are strongly developed there is much less need for bureaucratic control – indeed it would be counter-productive.

SUMMARY

The chapter discussed two of the most important decisions to be made in any organization: 'How decentralized should the organization be?' and 'What decisions should be delegated?'

There is no clear dividing-line between centralization and decentralization. One can only talk about organizations as being more or less centralized or decentralized. The simplest way of comparing the relative centralization of different organizations is by asking who makes the final decisions on specific subjects, and what sum of money requires board sanction; research workers have suggested other measures. Yet these formal measures do not tell us how much central control is exercised by means of indoctrination in company values.

The amount of decentralization that a management adopts will depend on a variety of factors. Management philosophy will be important. Top managers may believe in the virtues of decentralization or in the merits of centralization. A very large organization will find it harder to work successfully with a policy of centralization; well-established procedures and a common management outlook will make it easier to decentralize without losing control. The diversity of the organization's activities, the rate of change affecting it and the calibre of its staff are all relevant to deciding how much decentralization there should be.

The advantages and disadvantages of centralization or decentralization are described. In very general terms centralization improves control, decentralization makes for flexibility and encourages a sense of responsibility and the use of initiative. Yet despite all the research into decentralization, the evidence of its effects on performance are contradictory. One cannot simply take decentralization on its own and say what its effects on performance will be. Hence there is no clear answer to managers who want to know whether a decentralized policy is wise.

Top management has to decide what to delegate and to whom. It should concentrate itself on the decisions that are most vital for the organization. A number of criteria for deciding where decisions should be taken are described. Sometimes a knowledge of the local situation may be vital, while for other decisions a view of the wider implications for the organization as a whole will be needed. Management should consider where decisions ought to be taken, but it should remember that what happens in practice may be very different from what it thinks or plans; it can be salutary to check on where and how decisions are actually being made.

The analogy of a federal organization has recently been suggested as a way of thinking about how a large organization should manage its constituent parts.

Centralizing decision-taking is only one of the means by which top management can try to exercise control. It can also do so measuring performance against standards and targets and by establishing rules and procedures. The culture of an organization can, by its influence on how people think and act, be another powerful means of control.

NOTES

1. In some large companies decentralization may mean the establishment of subsidiary companies with responsibility for their own profit and loss. Delegation then takes place within the subsidiary companies, with only the profit and loss responsibility being delegated by the parent company.
2. Ernest Dale, *Organization* (New York: American Management Association, 1967) ch. 6.
3. D. S. Pugh, D. J. Hickson, C. R. Hinings and C. Turner, 'Dimensions of Organization Structure', *Administrative Science Quarterly*, vol. 13, no. 1 (June 1968) pp. 65–105.
4. Herbert Kaufman, *The Forest Ranger: A Study in Administrative Behaviour* (Baltimore, Md: Johns Hopkins University Press, 1960).

5.   Charles Perrow, 'Is Business Really Changing?', *Organizational Dynamics,*
     Summer 1974, p. 40.
6.   Peter Jennergren, 'Decentralization in Organizations', in Paul C. Nystrom
     and William H. Starbuck, *Handbook of Organizational Design*, vol. 2
     (London: Oxford University Press, 1981) pp. 39–59, reviews the research
     into decentralization to that date.
7.   Hilary Ingham, 'Organizational Structure and Internal Control in the UK
     Insurance Industry', *Services Industry Journal*, vol. 11, no. 4 (October 1991).
8.   Harold J. Leavitt and Thomas Whisler, 'Management in the 1980s', *Harvard
     Business Review*, Nov.–Dec. 1959, pp. 41–8.
9.   Charles Handy, *The Age of Unreason* (London: Business Books, 1989); and
     James O'Toole and Warren Bennis, 'Our Federalist Future', *California
     Management Review*, Summer 1992, pp. 73–90.
10. O'Toole and Bennis, 'Our Federalist Future'.
11. Christopher Lorenz, 'Fashionable Federalism', *Financial Times*, 18 Dec.
     1992, p. 9.
12. John Child, *Organization: A Guide to Problems and Practice*, 2nd edn (New
     York: Harper & Row, 1984) pp. 158–65.

9 Order versus Flexibility

We saw in the last chapter that the problem is to strike the right balance between centralization and decentralization, rather than to regard these as alternatives. The same is true for another important aspect of organizations, the degree of formalization. This means the establishment, usually in writing, of definite policies and procedures. Formalization is also characterized by a reliance on written rather than oral means of communication. As the title of this chapter suggests, the choice that has to be made is between the relative advantages of order and flexibility. These two can be seen as the opposite ends of the scale of formalization – the more formalization, the more order and the less flexibility. No organization can successfully set order as its overriding aim, nor can any put flexibility as its prime concern. All organizations need elements of both, and the problem is to decide what is the appropriate balance between them. The aim of this chapter is to help managers to make this decision so that they can tell when it is desirable to formalize and when formalization may have gone too far. Another way of putting this is the distinction between loose and tight. Some activities in an organization should be loose, that is they should be left up to the individuals and groups to decide what they should be doing to meet the current conditions; others should be tight, that is they need rules and procedures which should be carefully monitored.

A particular organization, especially if it is a large one, may be much more formalized in some parts than in others. This may be the result of deliberate design in order to meet obviously different conditions or it may be an unplanned reaction to the problems of dealing with different circumstances. Within the armed services, for example, long-established units may be more formalized and more hierarchical than those concerned with newer activities.

Formalization starts with the establishment of policy decisions – 'establishment' being in itself a word that suggests formality, as does 'procedure'. In businesses that are expanding, the managing director's life can be rendered intolerable by the requests for decisions unless policies are established that tell staff what to do or within what limits they can make a decision. Some kind of sales policy, for example, soon becomes necessary. Who should get discounts? Is it a customer who buys a certain quantity? One who pays cash? One whom one wants to tempt away from a competitor? One of the employees or a friend of the boss? And so on. The

115

managing director can come to a decision on each case as it comes up, he can leave things, either intentionally or by default, to the discretion of the staff, or he can formulate a policy to tell them which categories of people are to get discounts. Even in the last situation, however, there will be cases that the policy does not cover, and so the managing director will also have to give the sales manager some guidance as to when to use his own discretion and when he should refer back.

In what areas is it sensible for the chief to make policy decisions? There must be sufficient continuity and similarity in the types of decisions to be taken that a policy can cover most of them. For example, discounts could be given both to customers buying more than a certain quantity and to those paying cash, while terms for unusually large orders may need to be decided individually. The extent to which it is desirable for the managing director to establish policies will depend, in part, on how rapidly the business environment is changing. If the market is very competitive and changing rapidly, marketing policies will need to be reviewed frequently and much more discretion may have to be given to the person on the spot. It will, therefore, be less advantageous to establish policies. For a product with a relatively stable market, however, like refined sugar, marketing policies will only need to be reviewed infrequently, when something happens to disturb the market. For products like washing machines, that have a more fluctuating market, marketing policies can be established but will need to be reviewed more often.

Top management can formulate policies, but this does not necessarily mean that they will be carried out. It is important to remember that organizations are usually less formalized in practice than a description of the formal organization would suggest. Management at head office may describe company policy in considerable detail to a visiting research worker, but discussions with management in the field often show that this policy bears little or no resemblance to what happens in practice. This is true in all kinds of organizations, the gap between head office policy and the practice in the field being revealed by many government inquiries. What operating managers are doing in practice is likely to be a lot less tidy than the scheme devised in the relative peace of head office, whether it is the procedure to be followed in filling a vacant post, safety regulations to be adhered to or the policy to be adopted when deciding on the selling price. One large company designed a sophisticated method for deciding what quantities of each product the sales department should aim to sell, and at what prices. A manager from head office, on a field trip, found out, almost by chance, that what the salespeople actually did was to give whatever discount they though necessary to get the business. This action upset the validity of the careful calculations made at head office on the relative profitabilities of different products.

ADVANTAGES OF FORMALIZATION

Clarity of Policy

A clear statement of policy should give subordinates *more* freedom of action, although this is often not understood. Subordinates who are given no policies to guide their actions may appear to have great freedom, but they may instead feel inhibited by the knowledge that their boss will hold them responsible for whatever they do, even though they are not sure what is wanted. One senior civil servant at a seminar described how he felt freer to take decisions when he knew the minister's mind. With a minister whose wishes were less clear, he felt that he had to check back more frequently.

The clear formulation of policy has a further advantage: it stimulates management thinking. It requires an analysis both of objectives and of the best ways to achieve them, and this in turn can help management to think more critically about what it is doing. It is all too easy to think only vaguely, if at all, about what the policies should be.

Security or Certainty

Closely allied to clarity of policy is the advantage that comes from knowing what to expect. Clearly stated policies, formal procedures and rules can tell both employees and clients not only what they can and cannot do, but also what they will receive. Employees know their holiday entitlement and when they will have to retire; the citizen knows what is the rate of taxation – the abolition of arbitrary taxation was one of the early demands of parliamentarians; the customer knows how much discount will be given for cash.

Formalization also provides another type of security, that which comes from knowing what to do. This is most valuable in conditions of stress, in that it provides a known framework to help the individual cope with a frightening situation. This is one reason why the armed services and hospitals are more formalized than most businesses. An additional advantage is that it is easier to fit in when one moves in a highly formalized organization than it is in an organization where one knows less what to expect.

Temperamentally, people vary in the value that they attach to security and certainty. A few people thrive best in a freewheeling atmosphere, but most people are happiest where there is some structure to tell them what they should do, and some feel unhappy unless there is a very clearly defined structure.

Speed and Efficiency

Those who equate formalization with red tape will think it odd, even laughable, to say that it can make for speed and efficiency. Yet formal procedures can economize both on the time that must be spent considering what to do and the time it takes to do it. Once the best method of doing something has been worked out, it can be established as a formal procedure. People get used to doing things in this prescribed way and can become very efficient at doing so. All that is needed is an occasional review to check that it still is the best method. Good formal procedures can thus make for speed and efficiency while, in contrast, bad ones can be cumbersome and time-consuming, as we all know.

Control

The establishment of formal procedures for carrying out different tasks helps to ensure predictability of performance and thus to improve control. In large organizations it is common to establish procedures, for example, for filling vacancies, requisitioning stores and paying travelling expenses, but the extent to which these are formalized varies greatly. In one organization there will be the most detailed procedures laid down for every step in the process of filling a vacant job; in another, just as large, there will be no common procedures, each establishment developing its own, which may be comparatively informal.

The degree of formalization depends, in part, on the importance attached to control. In the public services this is usually greater than in private business, because of the requirement of public accountability. Government departments have to have more control, and hence more formalized procedures than do companies.

Equity

Formalization of personnel policies and of methods of dealing with clients can ensure that people get the same treatment; for example, all employees who have worked for a year get so many weeks' sick pay, men retire at 65, women at 60, and so on. Similarly, the number of days holiday per year may be specified, together with any differences for senior staff or for length of service. Such decisions are no longer left to the discretion of the boss.

The main advantage of such formalization is that it ensures similar treatment for all those who fit the rules. What will happen is predictable: the nurse knows what is to be done with a deceased patient's belongings. This certainly not only protects the person who has to administer the rules from the pressures of special pleading, but also protects the individual from the personal biases of officials and superiors.

DISADVANTAGES OF FORMALIZATION

We said at the beginning that order and flexibility can be seen as opposite ends of a line drawn to represent different degrees of formalization. The advantages of formalization are predominantly those associated with order. The disadvantages are mainly, but not solely, those of inflexibility.

Discourages Initiative

This is the reverse of the coin of predictability of performance. The aim of such predictability is to discourage initiative, such initiative being undesirable when you are in a clear position to predict what performance you want. However, this will often not be possible; circumstances may vary too much or change too frequently for it to be sensible to establish a formal procedure. Formal procedures are designed to deal with unchanging circumstances, or with a number of alternatives that can be specified in advance; they can be more of a handicap than a help when people have to deal with unforeseen situations.

The danger of discouraging initiative is that people with only moderate initiative may lose even that if they have never had occasion to exercise it at work. Those more strongly endowed will probably leave the organization because they find it too restricting.

It should not be assumed that all formalization discourages initiative. We saw in the discussion of advantages that the formulation of policy can provide the framework within which staff know that they can exercise initiative; where this is so they may feel freer to do so.

Promotes Evasion

The cynic could maintain that all formalization actively encourages initiative rather than the reverse. Human beings become very adept at finding ways round rules and procedures if they think that it is in their interest to do so. The deviser of rules and procedures needs to remember this fact and should try not to set rules that are an incentive to deception – tax officials, for example, need no such warning!

Handicaps Adaptation to Change

People who rely on following formal procedures tend to get set in their ways. If circumstances change they may be slow to realize it and slow to adapt. Those who are used to doing things one way often resent having to change to another way. People who are used to varying conditions are more likely to adjust easily to changes than those who are used to a stable environment.

Insensitivity

Equity was described as one of the advantages of formalization. Insensitivity is the other side of the picture, since it is difficult to devise rules that take account of all situations. To guard against this danger, some discretion is allowed; for example, to local officials in the rules governing supplementary social security payments.

FORMALIZATION IN PRACTICE

Retirement policies are a good example of some of the advantages and disadvantages of formalization. Retirement is something that can easily be formalized, as age can be the automatic criterion of when people should retire. One of the merits of formalization, as we saw, is certainty: people know what to expect. It is also an easier policy to administer than one that leaves discretion to the individual. This ease and certainty, though, is achieved at the expense of flexibility. A person's age, as studies of ageing have shown, is a very crude guide to the decline in usefulness. People age at different rates, so that one person of 65 may be physically and mentally younger than another of 60. Even amongst those who age at the same rate, some contribute much more to organizations than others. Many organizations try to have retirement policies that make provision for early retirement, either voluntary or compulsory. They may also, as in the Civil Service, have a provision so that, although everyone retires at a fixed age, some can be invited to stay on for a further period. Such retirement policies aim to secure some flexibility so that some retire earlier and a few later than the majority, while all the time retaining most of the advantages of certainty.

Managers need to weigh the advantages and disadvantages of formalization. Usually, it is not a simple question of deciding for or against rules or
procedures, but rather of deciding how general or how specific and detailed
they should be. Formalization can be a handicap in rapidly changing conditions and where initiative from the person on the spot is essential. It is
most useful where uniform performance is important, as it is where safety
needs protecting.

An example of the need for tight management, where more formalization was required, is given in the Report of the Court of Formal Investigation into the capsizing of the car ferry, *Herald of Free Enterprise*, outside
the Belgian port of Zeebrugge in March 1987, with large loss of life and
many injuries. It was found that the ship had left with her bow doors open
which caused her to capsize rapidly. The report, by the Hon. Mr Justice
Sheen, said:

> The Board of Directors did not appreciate their responsibility for the safe
> management of their ships. They did not apply their minds to the
> question: What orders should be given for the safety of our ships?

> . . . All concerned in management, from the members of the Board of
> Directors down to the junior superintendents, were guilty of fault in that
> all must be regarded as sharing responsibility for the failure of
> management. From top to bottom the body corporate was infected with
> the disease of sloppiness. . . It is only necessary to quote one example of
> how the standard of management fell short . . .

> On 18th March 1986 there was a meeting of Senior Masters with
> management, at which Mr Develin was in the chair [Chief Marine
> Superintendent and a Director of the Company which owned *Herald of
> Free Enterprise*]. One of the topics raised for discussion concerned the
> recognition of the Chief Officer as Head of Department and the roles of the
> Maintenance Master and Chief Officer. Mr Develin said, although he was
> still considering writing definitions of these different roles, he felt 'it was
> preferable not to define the roles but to allow them to evolve'. That
> attitude . . . demonstrates an inability or unwillingness to give clear orders.
> Clear instructions are the foundation of a safe system of operation.

> It was the failure to give clear instructions about the duties of the officers
> on the Zeebrugge run which contributed so greatly to the cause of the
> disaster.[1]

A failure to ensure tight management where that is needed can, as Hon.
Mr Justice Sheen said, lead to sloppiness. However, job definition, rules

and procedures are not in themselves sufficient to ensure that all will go as prescribed. As Lord Cullen said in his review in 1990 of the explosion on the oil rig, Piper Alpha:[2]

> Occidental Petroleum Management should have been more aware of the need for a high standard of incident prevention and fire fighting. They were too easily satisfied that the permit to work system was being operated correctly, relying on the absence of any feedback of problems as indicating that all was well.

There needs to be a good monitoring system as well and supports at all levels for the aims of the procedures. In yet another accident report, that on the fire at King's Cross underground station,[3] Desmond Fennel Qc said:

> The chairman of London Regional Transport . . . told me that whereas financial matters were strictly monitored, safety was not . . . in my view he was mistaken as to his responsibilities.

It can be very difficult to introduce new ways of thinking and new approaches to problems into an organization which is highly formalized. Instead it may be easier and faster to set up a new organization. The use of project groups is one way of doing this on a small scale. In government the setting up of a new department is a more drastic attempt to achieve a new approach, free from a long-established departmental viewpoint.

TYPES OF FORMALIZATION

We have talked about formalization in general. It will be useful now to look at the different types of formalization so that we can examine their specific advantages and disadvantages. There are eight main types, but not all of them will be found in every organization.

Rules

This is the common type of formalization. All except the very smallest organizations have rules. In some they may be written down and handed to each new employee, posted on notice boards or included in organization manuals. In others they may be traditional rules that are well known but have never been written down.

Most people would accept the need for rules, although most would at times decry them as 'stupid red tape' or 'bureaucracy gone mad'. The inappropriateness of many rules, and the extent to which they are ignored, is highlighted whenever employees start 'working to rule'. The commuter who hopes to get home punctually by his or her usual train learns at such times that working to rule can cause aggravating delays. We know all too well that rules – at least those drawn up by other people – can be stupid. We know, too, that rules can proliferate as their authors try and deal with all the different ways that people have found of getting round them.

What are we to do, though? Abolish all rules? That is not a long-term answer, though it is a way of starting afresh. The best we can do is to be aware of the dangers, to make few rules and to make them as clear as we can. We should also try and design rules that, as far as possible, are likely to be accepted as sensible. To achieve this it can be helpful to consult the people who are going to be asked to keep the rules.

This discussion has so far concerned itself with internally imposed rules, but for all organizations there are also externally imposed rules. Members of the New York Stock Exchange, for example, must operate within voluminous and stringent Stock Exchange rules, which means that firms must perforce be highly formalized.

Formal Procedures

Formal procedures are those that are officially established. They detail how certain activities should be carried out, such as the procedures to be followed in a fire drill. Any organization will develop a large number of procedures in order to ensure that certain tasks are carried out in a uniform way. Formal procedures can be overdone, but many managers err in the other direction by paying too little attention to the need to systematize work.

Organization Charts

This is a common method of formalization, although not universal, since some companies think that such charts can be more misleading than helpful. The usual type of chart, as in Figure 9.1, highlights the vertical and departmental relationships, but not the horizontal ones: it gives no indication of differences in status of managers shown on the same level; it tends to show what the structure is supposed to be, rather than what it is. Additionally, it can rapidly get out of date, and so companies that take their charts seriously frequently have to issue new ones or amendment sheets. In a large rapidly-changing organization this can result in a big increase in inter-office paper.

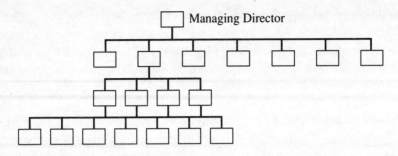

Figure 9.1 *Traditional Organization Chart*
(this is an abbreviated and simplified example; many organization charts
are both voluminous and complex)

While charts have their limitations, they are still a useful tool. It would be hard to have a management succession policy in a large organization without the help of such charts. They are especially useful to the new employee, the training department and the visiting research worker as a starting-point for understanding or explaining the formal structure. Drawing up an organization chart can also help to show up defects in the structure, and stimulate management to give more thought to what form of organization is appropriate.

Organization Manuals

Organization charts are sometimes supplemented in large organizations by organization manuals. These may simply be in the form of brief notes, accompanying the departmental charts, explaining the functions of each department and its relationships with other departments. At the opposite extreme they may consist of volumes which detail the responsibilities and authority of different posts and the procedures to be adopted in carrying out different tasks. Clearly the latter approach is only appropriate where a high degree of control is both desirable and practicable, for example as with some government departments.

Job Descriptions and Job Specification

These were discussed in Chapter 2, on the division of work. They are mentioned again here because they are one of the common types of formalization.

Memoranda, Minutes and Files

The more formalized the organization, the more communications will be written rather than spoken. Written communications provide a record that can be referred to later, this being especially important in the public service, for example where questions in Parliament have to be answered. It can be important, too, where the people involved do not trust each other and want to be able to refer to a record. The written word is likely to be more carefully considered than the spoken, so it encourages people to think before they write. Unfortunately they may not express themselves clearly and misunderstandings are less easily cleared up than during a conversation. Written communications can take less time than spoken ones; it depends both on what has to be communicated and on the individuals involved.

Sometimes there is no practical choice between writing or talking – fire-fighting, for example, does not wait for written messages. The greater the uncertainty as to what is going to happen or what should be done, the more likely managers are to talk to each other rather than to write.

Managing change requires leadership and leadership is primarily exercised by talking – and listening; rarely by writing. This truth is one that some top managers in the public sector find hard to learn. They seek to enlist commitment to major changes, but yet still circulate a mass of paper about management changes. Expressing one's views on paper rather than in person can become a habit that is hard to unlearn.

Committees

The committee, as distinct from the formal group discussion, is one of the distinguishing features of a formalized organization. Committees can be described as discussion groups that have an agenda and which keep minutes. They may also have voluminous papers for each item on the agenda. A good committee secretary can do much to save the time of committee members and to clarify decision making.

The pros and cons of committees were discussed in Chapter 4 on Coordination.

Appointment Diaries

A doubtful addition to the list, but perhaps worth including as another method of formalization, are appointment diaries. The ease with which one can talk to a manager varies considerably from one organization to another.

It also varies, of course, with the manager's position; the more senior the post the more likely she is to have a secretary to make appointments. It varies, too, with individuals, depending on freedom of choice; they can seek to formalize discussions with others by specifying time and duration or they can adopt an open-door policy. Organizations may make their own rules about how freely available their managers should be. However, there are also cultural differences. Protecting oneself with a secretary and an engagement book is a type of formalization that tends to be frowned on in the United States; in contrast, managers in some European countries attach great importance to the respect that is shown by making an appointment.

Rank and Status Symbols

The more formalized the organization, the more likely it is to have formal symbols of rank and status. One purpose of these symbols is to strengthen formal authority by increasing the social distance between one level and another. There are disadvantages in doing this, as we saw in Chapter 5 on Superior–Subordinate Relationships.

The armed services have uniforms with distinctive badges of rank; in nursing there used to be different uniforms for each grade of nurse and nursing officer. Now these are rare, though they still remain in a few hospitals. Industry and civil administration usually have no prescribed clothes for distinguishing ranks, but almost all have some formal rank and status symbols, apart from the informal symbols that tend to flourish; there are many examples, such as the size and furnishings of an office, and what lavatories, lifts or car parks one can use. In the United States, the level you occupy in the office building is usually a reliable guide to your position in the hierarchy; this is not the case in the United Kingdom, even in the new skyscrapers, though directors are often found at the top. In Britain, the form of address adopted used to be important, especially in the more formalized organizations; in hospitals, for example, the nursing staff were traditionally addressed by their job – nurse, sister, matron. Now this is rare. Christian names have become common, as they have in most organizations. But practice still varies in different hospitals; in some the Christian name will be prefixed by the rank, for example, Sister Mary.

CONCLUSIONS

The most appropriate balance between order and flexibility shifts in a time of rapid change such as exists today and which is likely to continue. It is still sensible to systematize where that can usefully be done. Some committees will still be required, particularly in the public sector. But the prime need is for more flexibility so that managers and front line staff can respond quickly to changes. This means talking rather than writing, impromptu meetings between those who are relevant to a particular problem, and project groups rather than periodic committees with their dangers of attendance for status reasons.

Formalization has great advantages. Many British organizations probably do not have enough of it; managers muddle along instead of thinking how to systematize what they do. However, formalization, as we have seen, has its dangers. They are greatest when management fails to review the appropriateness of rules and procedures and the usefulness of paperwork and committees. Management should frequently ask itself 'What is the purpose of this?' Periodic spring-cleans – one of the functions of an O&M department – are necessary to clear away the accretions of the past, the forms that are no longer needed, the reports that no one reads, the rules that no longer apply or that no longer should apply, the procedures that are not suited to the changed conditions, the committees that have outlived their purpose. Successful formalization needs an actively inquiring mind, one that asks 'How can we organize this best?' and one that frequently questions the current relevance of past answers.

SUMMARY

The degree of formalization is one of the scales by which organizations can be compared. A very formalized organization is one with many rules and formal procedures, where written communication is often used in preference to the spoken word.

Some formalization is essential in all but the smallest organization. There must be some policies to provide for consistency in decisions and some procedures to make for smooth administration. Management's problem is to decide how much formalization is desirable.

The main advantages of formalization is that is makes for order by clarifying policy, by creating the security that comes from knowing what to expect and what to do, and by improving control. It can make for greater speed and efficiency, provided the rules and procedures are designed sensibly and not allowed to get out of date. It also ensures the equitable treatment of categories of people.

Its disadvantages are those of inflexibility. It can discourage useful initiatives and encourage attempts to get round the rules. It can handicap adaptation to change. Rules designed to fit broad categories of people can cause hardship when applied to specific cases.

The main types of formalization are rules, formal procedures, organization charts and manuals, job descriptions and job specifications, memoranda, minutes and files, committees, appointment diaries and symbols of rank and status. Their utility and their dangers were discussed. The values of formalization should not be ignored even in a time of rapid change, but the desirable balance has shifted towards more flexibility.

NOTES

1. Hon. Mr Justice Sheen, *Herald of Free Enterprise. Report of Court No. 8074 Formal Investigation* (London: Her Majesty's Stationery Office, 1987) p. 14.
2. Hon. Lord Cullen, *The Public Enquiry into the Piper Alpha Disaster*, 2 vols (London: Her Majesty's Stationery Office, 1990) vol. 1, p. 3.
3. D. Fennel, *The Investigation into the King's Cross Underground Fire* (London: Her Majesty's Stationery Office, 1988) p. 17.

10 The Changing Organization

Organizations are not islands that can live unto themselves, ignoring the world around them. They are shaped by their environment and in turn help to shape it. The purpose of this chapter is to look at this interaction and to try and understand the ways in which organizations are changing.

EXTERNAL CHANGES AFFECTING ORGANIZATIONS

1. one world;
2. development of the EC;
3. state intervention;
4. rapid technical change;
5. social changes,
6. consumerism.

These changes alter the environment within which all organizations must operate. It used to be companies that were most vulnerable to external changes, but it is arguable whether that is still true. Companies are often more vulnerable than they used to be, but other organizations, particularly those in the public sector, are now much affected by external changes. It is only the first two of the six changes that affect business more than the public and voluntary sectors.

One World

This is not true politically but it is increasingly true economically, culturally and commercially. Fast transport and worldwide communications reduce cultural differences. Increasingly, cities look like each other, as do clothes and transport of people who live in them. What they eat and drink differs more, but some brand products are found in every continent – Coca-Cola, Schweppes tonic water and Gordon's gin, for example.

Companies in one country are increasingly affected by what happens in other countries, the strongest competition often coming from companies abroad. The rapid development of the Far Eastern economies has contributed to the decline of traditional manufacturing industries in Western countries; what has happened to British shipbuilding is but one example of the impact of foreign competition. Companies are also vulnerable to changes in the world economy and to political decisions in other countries, the oil crises in the 1970s and the exchange speculation affecting EC currencies in the early 1990s and the foreign and economic policies pursued by US administrations being but a few examples of this vulnerability.

The development of a worldwide market is taking place in a world in which many more independent countries are wanting to control their own economies. Companies operating from overseas are frequently viewed with suspicion, particularly in developing countries. Selling in a foreign market now often means establishing or acquiring a subsidiary there, which in turn introduces new management problems for companies that had previously operated only from their home base: problems of managing at a distance in a culture that may not be understood; problems of dealing with foreign governments and great political uncertainties.

Even within the public sector there is more interest in what is happening in the public sector overseas. The reorganization of the National Health Service, for example, was modelled on ideas from the US, and its progress is of interest elsewhere.

Development of the EC

All organizations in EC countries are affected by EC regulations; companies, of course, most of all because of the achievement of the common market, but legal, social and environmental regulations affect all organizations. Changes in health and safety requirements are the ones that many have found most onerous. Equal opportunity regulations are also having widespread effects. In the case of the UK, for example, the European Court has ruled that women should not be discriminated against by being made to retire earlier than male employees.

A lesson that the Confederation of British Industry (CBI) in Britain has been trying to put across is that companies should be active in the relevant EC groups so that they have a chance to influence the early stages of formulating new regulations. This is one of many examples of the need for top management in any organization to be active in trying to influence its environment, rather than just react later to what has taken place.

State Intervention

State intervention has been a major factor affecting organizations for many years. The aims of the intervention have developed and partially changed over time. Initially, governments were primarily concerned with establishing the rules within which businesses should operate. These rules are frequently added to, or changed. In many countries laws against monopolies have long been an important aspect of 'holding the ring'. Increasingly, governments are also concerned with the management process itself, both in companies and in the public service. The British government, whichever party has been in power, has sought for ways of improving the efficiency of industry and of stimulating exports, its efforts having ranged widely from providing finance to encouraging amalgamations, in the hope that bigger units would be able to compete more effectively in the international market, and to giving honours for business success.

In the 1980s a new approach to the public sector was adopted in the UK which continued into the 1990s. It relied more upon market pressures to promote efficiency. This had always been the aim behind anti-monopoly legislation, but now the market was seen as a way of improving the efficiency of the public sector and of making it more responsive to consumers. Where feasible, state-run industries were privatized. The same philosophy also resulted in major organizational changes in other parts of the public sector. The division of the NHS into purchasers and providers and the encouragement of trust hospitals, responsible for their own activities within the overall control of the centre, is one example of this change in approach. Compulsory tendering in the public sector for some services was an earlier example. The partial hiving-off of parts of the Civil Service into agencies is yet another. Early examples of agencies were Her Majesty's Stationery Office and the Civil Service College; but later, more mainstream government activities which provided a service were also made agencies. Creation of an agency, headed by a chief executive, was intended to give it greater autonomy and to make it more accountable for its performance.

Governments, and top management too, tend to overestimate the effects of changes in the ownership and structure of organizations. Many of the same people necessarily remain and they carry with them many of their previous attitudes. Nor can all the systems be radically changed or chaos would result. Hence the disappointments that are experienced in major changes. This was true, in the late 1940s and the 1950s, of the impact of nationalization which had been expected to transform the way employees felt about working in an industry. It has often been true of the results of privatization and of the creation of agencies. A study by Hickson and

McMillan in 1981 of 46 diverse public- and private-sector organizations may provide an explanation. They found that it was the size of the organization and the extent of its dependence upon other organizations that determined its form more than its ownership.[1]

Rapid Technical Change

The rapid rate of technical change has altered the tempo of the environment within which organizations must live. To survive in this rapidly changing world they must adapt faster.

One of the main impacts of technical change on companies is the high rate of product obsolescence. In the past if a company developed a good product it could expect to go on selling it for many years. Now few products are invulnerable to the effects of technical change, and hence many companies must devote large sums to research and development and to market research. Material substitution may change the character of an industry or make it obsolete. The development of new products may replace others, as television partly replaced the cinema. New models can rapidly supersede earlier ones. Companies that do not keep up lose their sales.

The most pervasive technical changes affecting all organizations are those stemming from computers and other aspects of information technology, such as the fax. ('Information technology' is the term used for any technology that captures, stores, transmits, processes or presents information electronically.) Three different ways in which information technology is affecting some organizations, and will affect many more, have become clear. The first and often the most important effect on some companies is that information technology changes the ways in which the product is delivered and the kinds of services that can be provided. An example is the delivery of financial services both for companies and for the individual customer. A second change, and the one that received most attention in predictions, is that IT affects the quality, nature and speed of the information that can be provided. Where it is used effectively it can also provide a competitive advantage to those companies which improve their efficiency by doing so. This kind of change also applies to all forms of organization, whether public or private. The third kind of change also applies to all kinds of organizations, and concerns the considerable cost not just of the equipment, but of its maintenance and of the software. These costs can be frightening and are a stimulus to cooperation, even between competitors.

Social Changes

Social changes, like state intervention, are a continuing external factor to which all organizations must adapt. The growth of a better educated population has been one of the major changes of the century which has affected organizations in many ways, such as management style and recruitment policies. One of the more recent effects has been the growth of market segmentation to meet educated consumers' distinctive wants. Yet another on-going change is that in the ethnic mix of the population, particularly in certain localities.

The most recent social changes to affect organizations are the pressures for equal opportunities and for employment policies that take account of family obligations. The growing concern for the environment and for actions to restrict pollution and to limit the destruction of natural habitats is another recent social change to which managements must adapt.

Demographic changes also affect organizations. Changes in the relative proportion of potential employees of different ages influence recruitment patterns and market opportunities. New market opportunities, for example, are created by the growing number of old people: for organized holidays for those who are still active and, later, for nursing homes for those in need of residential care.

Consumerism

The rise of consumerism is one of the effects of a better educated, and hence more demanding, population. It is facilitated by faster and more widespread communication. It is also a by-product of the major shift from predominantly manufacturing industries to service industries. In service industries companies compete by satisfying the consumer.

CHANGES WITHIN ORGANIZATIONS

The changes affecting organizations have caused organizations themselves to change. The main ways in which they have changed are as follows:

1. increasing size;
2. the shrinking organization;
3. the growth of the international corporation;
4. more fluid boundaries;
5. changes in staff composition;

6. changing career patterns.

Increasing Size

When this book was first written in 1970, increasing size was described as
the most striking change in companies in different parts of the world. This
is no longer true, particularly in the developed world. A variety of reasons,
discussed below, have caused many companies, and the public services, to
shrink. Some companies, of course, continue to grow via acquisitions and
mergers, while others grow mainly or wholly by internal growth. The
achievement of the Common Market has stimulated cross-country acquisitions and alliances within the EC.

The pressures to grow can be strong. These were well expressed in
Hewlett-Packard's *Statement of Corporate Objectives* of May 1979:[2]

> We do not believe that large size is important for its own sake; however,
> for at least two basic reasons, continuing growth is essential for us to
> achieve our other objectives.
>
> In the first place, we serve a rapidly growing and expanding segment
> of our technological society. To remain static would be to lose ground.
> We cannot maintain a position of strength and leadership in our fields
> without growth.
>
> In the second place, growth is important in order to attract and hold
> high calibre people. These individuals will align their future only with a
> company that offers them considerable opportunity for personal
> progress. Opportunities are greater and more challenging in a growing
> company.

These are arguments for growth. They remain valid arguments even
though they became impractical for many companies in the recession of the
late 1980s and early 1990s. Then Hewlett Packard was but one of many
examples of IT companies who had to adjust to changes in the computer
industry as well as to the recession.

There are also advantages in being a large company. In a technical industry it is easier to finance the necessary research and development to keep
pace with, or ahead of, competitors in the search for improved products. In
many industries there are economies to be achieved by large-scale production. Increasingly, with the growth of a world market, there are economies,
too, to be gained by a larger selling base. Finally, there is the defensive
advantage, in that a large organization is less likely to be taken over. The
threat of acquisition exists for all but the very largest companies. In some
industries the aim is to create large enough units to compete internationally.

The increase in size that took place in organizations until the late 1970s was most marked in business and government services, but it was also found elsewhere. Farms became larger, as did hospitals and schools. The large new district general hospitals in Britain were due, at least in part, to the increasing cost of medical services; large hospitals can more economically support the range of medical services and the expensive equipment that are needed. To be bigger is still seen as an advantage for some activities; farms and retail chain stores continue to get larger, though smaller ones can remain profitable.

There are also many disadvantages in being big. The problems of organization become more complex and take up more of management's time, and it is harder to achieve the right balance between order and flexibility or between centralization and decentralization. Human relations problems also tend to be greater in large organizations; increasing size is often necessary for economic reasons, but in many ways it makes managers' lives more difficult. The reverse trend to smaller organizations thus has advantages, so as the move to smaller establishments within large organizations.

The Shrinking Organization

The main reason for the decline in the numbers employed in many large companies, particularly manufacturing companies, was the recessions which started in 1979 and again ten years later. The decline in markets and strong competition both from home and abroad meant that companies and some of the nationalized industries had to reduce output and seek to improve productivity. The redundancies were large, as unemployment figures testified. Another important reason was the move, discussed earlier, of hiving-off or subcontracting non-core activities. How drastically this can shrink an organization is illustrated by the privatized Yorkshire Water which decided in 1992 that 21 of its 40 areas of business, or about 65 per cent of employees, could over time be put outside the core. This means that they must compete in the private sector or be closed.[3]

There are other longer-term reasons why organizations have had to shrink. These reasons act as a counterweight to the factors that encourage growth. For example, there is the continuing move to greater automation of many work processes, and the tendency to hive off some activities to other firms and to consultants. The problems that stem from being big mean that smaller companies may be able to provide a cheaper, and possibly a better, service. Information technology also makes it easier to use some previous full-time staff as part-time consultants.

Growth of the International Corporation

The other changes that we discuss can apply to any kind of organization; some apply mainly or wholly to large organizations and some to small ones too. However, this third change applies only to large companies.

Before 1950, oil companies were the main international corporations. From the 1950s onwards, companies in other industries had to become both more internationally minded and more international. The development of a worldwide consumer market opened up new opportunities for expansion, as did the international market for advanced technical equipment. The domestic markets of medium-sized countries like Britain are individually no longer large enough to support the cost of research and development in highly technical industries such as computers and aero engines; both must have foreign markets if they are to hope to pay their way.

International trading companies have existed for centuries, as have companies that marketed their products abroad. What is new is the great increase in the number of subsidiary and associated companies overseas, as well as the development of multinational companies. Now even medium-sized companies may have overseas subsidiaries to manufacture and sell their products. Indeed, local regulations may make this a prerequisite to selling their goods in that country.

The growth of the international corporation changes the ways in which its top managers think. Strategic thinking must be carried out on a worldwide basis, making the task of trying to optimize resources much more complex. Managers need an understanding of local politics and a sensitivity to cultural differences if they are to operate successfully in other countries. The oil companies have known this for a long time and, by virtue of this international approach, seemed in the past to be in a different class to other industries in their management thinking. Now more and more companies are having to learn the same lessons. The automobile industry is a more recent example of one that now optimizes its operations internationally, making components in different countries and assembling them in yet another.

Companies go through different stages on the way to becoming multinational corporations. The first step is the search for markets outside the home country. A company can earn the majority of its profits overseas and still remain a primarily national company in its outlook, although some of its managers will need to understand the requirements of foreign markets. The next stage is developing or acquiring overseas subsidiaries. The acquisition of a large foreign company can be a traumatic experience, because of the unexpected problems that may follow acquisition. This has been true for a number of large British companies in the USA, even though the close cultural links should have made it easier to understand what the potential problems were. (Although being sent overseas to sort out a loss-making foreign subsidiary can in itself be a powerful method of management development!) Joint ventures with a foreign company or government are another way of doing business overseas. Such ventures may be a free choice or a precondition of doing business at all. The range of such joint ventures can be very wide; a very large company can have more than a thousand.

Two further steps are necessary to become a truly multinational company. One is to think of the company's development in international rather than national terms, with all that implies regarding where goods are produced, where markets are sought, where taxes are paid and even where the head office is located. This means a shift in the kind of strategic thinking carried out regarding the company's future. The other step towards being multinational is a change in who does the thinking, that is in the composition of top management. At first all the top managers and most of the middle managers, too, will be from the country of the company's origin, British, American, German, Dutch or Swedish managers being sent overseas. Objections to expatriate managers in many countries then leads to the next stage, which is for foreign subsidiaries to be mainly or wholly staffed by local nationals. Next is the posting of home nationals overseas and of foreign managers to the head office as part of management development. A further stage of multinationalism is 'cross posting', where managers in foreign subsidiaries are posted to another country, not just to head office. A yet further step taken by a few companies, such as ICI, is to have members of other nationalities as part of the main board or in the major top management posts at the head office. This is likely to become more common and can contribute to developing a more international outlook. An even further stage of becoming truly international is to have a top management composed of managers from different countries and, perhaps even more radically, to appoint a chief executive from a different country.

All these steps still leave the headquarters in the country of origin, but that may be beginning to change too. A number of large companies have moved not their headquarters but the head office of one of their major global businesses to another country. The motive may be to be nearer the main customers or to foster international thinking and staffing. For example, Monsanto Resins, the second largest chemical division of the American chemical company, Monsanto, moved in early 1992 from St Louis in the US Midwest to Brussels. It is easier to think globally in a more international community like Brussels than in the centre of the US.[4] Where the

head office is in the country of origin and most of the business is outside
the country the danger is that the home country will still get too much
attention. This is a greater danger in a large country like the US than in
Sweden, whose international companies must be strongly international to
survive.

More Fluid Boundaries

The main effect of the environmental changes which we have described
is to make the boundaries of the organization more fluid; that is, to make
the departments and the organization itself less autonomous. Organizations, particularly those in business, are increasingly subject to external
influences. This means that management must be able to adjust faster
than in the past. To do so requires both a greater sensitivity to what is
happening in the world outside and a more flexible organization. One
aspect of flexibility is the variety of relationships that managers will have
with people in other parts of the organization. Another is the frequency of
organizational changes which in a classic article were likened to 'camping on seesaws'.[5]

Many more people in organizations have positions on the boundary with
the outside world than in the interwar period. Then it was primarily the
sales and purchasing departments that had to deal with people both inside
and outside the company; now many managers in other departments also
have external contacts. The fact that top managers may spend much of their
time with people from outside the organization is a reflection of how
important they are to the company's success. This is true for public service
organizations as well as for companies. For example, in the NHS the creation of healthy alliances was one of the prescriptions for helping to implement the reforms of the early 1990s.

It is not only that more people in an organization work with people outside it but that the relationships are becoming more mixed. Two Swedish
academics who study international business networks describe the changes
like this:

The international business arena is enlarging rapidly as well as
undergoing dramatic structural changes. The old international business
actors – large and small multinational firms engaged in industry, trade
and services – are expanding all over the world . . . New actors – private
and public – are entering . . . Sometimes the firms compete on their
own, sometimes they co-operate with other actors in ever changing

patterns. The traditional distinct roles in the market place as suppliers, customers and competitors are becoming mixed. Competitors in one market co-operate in another and are suppliers and customers to each other in a third. Correspondingly, traditional boundaries between industries are breaking down and firms from different industries meet in new markets.[6]

Changes in Staff Composition

The relative proportions of different types of staff have altered in many organizations. There are now far more knowledge workers, while automation has often decreased the number of manual and clerical workers. The result is a change in the shape of the traditional organizational pyramid, with many more people at the intermediate levels and fewer at the bottom. The problem of many managers is now that of managing those with professional and technical qualifications rather than that of managing manual workers. Another major change is the increase in the number of female employees, many of whom work part-time.[7]

Changing Career Patterns

Managers are moving between jobs, between organizations and between employment and self-employment much more than before. One reason for this is the increase in the proportion of staff who have professional and technical qualifications.

Professionalization has changed the reference-point for many employees. They look to their professional peers for judgement on their activities and often expect to get their promotion by moving to another organization. Their loyalty is to their profession rather than to their employer.

Another reason for changes in career patterns is the job insecurity that has come from the intense competitive pressure and from the changes in the public sector. Many people have had to move, others have chosen to move in a more open market-place for talent, yet others have moved to improve the look of their CV and hence their marketability.

The aim of developing managers with a wider knowledge of the business has led to greater mobility within companies. Hence horizontal movements are more common. Also the shorter hierarchy that now exists in many companies makes horizontal movement the main way of providing a variety of job experience.

LINKS BETWEEN ENVIRONMENTAL CHANGES AND CHANGES IN ORGANIZATIONS

Table 10.1 shows the relationships between the environmental changes described earlier and the changes that have taken place in organizations. The relationships between the two should be thought of as interacting, so that although the changes in organizations are due, in whole or in part, to the changes in the environment, some of the changes in organizations also have repercussions in the environment. Rapid technical change, for example, has helped to produce organizations like IBM, but such companies have also contributed, through their research, to technical change.

EXAMPLE 1: ICL

Not all the organizational changes that we described took place in every organization. A large company in a highly technical industry provides a good example of one that *is* affected by most of these changes. International Computers Ltd in the United Kingdom is such an example. Briefly, the history of this company is that it was created by successive mergers and later taken over, first by a British company and later by a Japanese. The first merger was in 1959 between Power-Samas and British Tabulating Machines, two punched-card machine companies. This merger, like the second one, took place primarily in order to pool research costs and to be in a stronger position to meet United States' competition. The new company, ICT (International Computers and Tabulators), still found it difficult to compete successfully with IBM, the huge American computer company. The Ministry of Technology, through the Industrial Expansion Act, therefore promoted a merger in 1968 between ICT and the computer division of English Electric, then the other main British computer manufacturer. The company continued to have difficulties in competing successfully against its international competitors, particularly IBM, and in 1984 was taken over by Standard Telephones and Cables.

The next major change was the sale of 80 per cent of ICL to Fujitsu in 1990. (In 1990 ICL was doing relatively well for its industry.) This was but one of many examples of disposals by large diversified companies facing financial problems. (The remaining 20 per cent is owned by the Canadian company, Northern Telecom.) Fujitsu is a Japanese company and one of the

Table 10.1 The Impact of Changes in the Environment on Changes in Organizations

Changes in environment	Resulting changes in organization					
	Increasing size	The shrinking organization	Growth of international corporations	More fluid boundaries	Changing composition of staff	Changing career patterns
One World	Yes	Yes	Yes	Yes	Yes	Yes
Development of the EC	Yes	Yes	–	Yes	Yes	Yes
State intervention	Yes	Yes	Yes	Yes	Yes	Yes
Rapid technical change	Yes	Yes	Yes	Yes	Yes	Yes
Social change	–	–	–	Yes	Yes	Yes
Consumerism	–	–	–	Yes	–	–

largest IT companies in the world. In its 1991 annual report Fujitsu explained the rationale of its acquisition as follows:

> After nearly a decade of technological cooperation, we welcome ICL into the Fujitsu Group. Our new relationship will make the cooperation even closer in terms of sharing resources in marketing, R&D and the promotion of open systems, in which ICL is especially strong. We expect synergy to grow from the recognition of and respect for differences in each company's culture, and from the areas of expertise Fujitsu and ICL bring to the partnership.
>
> . . . The Fujitsu–ICL partnership is unique in its concept of globalization. We believe that each country and each company has its own culture, and rather than color over the other to fit our own image we should live together respecting each other's differences and learning from each other's strengths.
>
> ICL continues to be run autonomously as a European-based information technology (IT) company.[8]

The recession of the early 1990s caused problems for many of the companies in the IT industry, including IBM and Fujitsu. The latter recorded its first ever loss in the first half of 1992.

Many different reasons have been given for the bumpy ride that has characterized the long history of ICL and its predecessors. A common explanation over the years was that the company was too small to compete effectively with international giants, particularly IBM; that was a major argument behind the government-sponsored merger of ICT and English Electric. However, the Harvard strategy writer Michael Porter, has argued that it is not large size but the existence of a number of national competitors that promotes efficiency.[9] This view would suggest that the British company had been too molly-coddled by the government and needed the kind of domestic competition faced by Japanese electronics companies. It may be that the EC will provide that.

ICL's history is an example of four of the changes affecting organizations described earlier: one world; development of the EC; state intervention; and technical change. It is now part of a global Japanese company, but its European base is also important. In 1988 it set up a European Strategy Board to plan the company's European policy so as to make the best use of the common market from the end of 1992. In its 1991 *Accounts and Review of Operations* ICL says that its vision is to be Europe's leading international information technology company and that it was continuing to make progress in realizing that vision. In 1991 its acquisitions included companies in Scandinavia and Holland.

The history of ICL and its predecessors is above all an example of the changes that companies have to make to adapt to technical change. The original companies started making punched cards before the need for office machinery was recognized. The first major success of one of the original companies was to get the contract for processing the 1911 Census. A recent history of the company by Campbell-Kelly said that it was the launch of the IBM 1401 in October 1959, and the start of volume deliveries in the winter of 1961–2, that led to the collapse of the punched-card industry.[10] Since then the computer industry has passed through major technical changes which have affected the relative fortunes of the different companies in the industry. The most important of these changes have been: the shift from large mainframe computers, housed in their own air conditioned environments, to small personal computers; the vastly increased speed of processing; and most recently, the shift in relative importance from computer manufacture to the provision of software. The last is illustrated in the early 1990s by the problems of IBM and the continuing successes of Microsoft. The fact that the industry has changed its name from computer to IT is itself a sign of the extent of the technical changes that have affected it. Managing in such an industry can rightly be described as challenging!

Table 10.2 summarizes the external changes that have affected ICL over the years, while Table 10.3 shows the organizational changes that have affected the company.

EXAMPLE 2: A GENERAL HOSPITAL

ICL is a company that should show more change than many other manufacturing companies, and even more than other types of organization, yet if we look at a very different type of organization – a general hospital in England – we will also be able to trace considerable changes. Table 10.4 shows the effects of environmental changes on the hospital, while Table 10.5 details the organizational changes. The analysis is limited to general hospitals in the UK because of the distinctive effects of government-imposed reorganizations, which vary in different countries.

Table 10.2   *External Changes Affecting ICL*

External changes	*Affected ICL or earlier, its constituent companies*
One world	Yes, the growing market for computers in different countries meant greater opportunities and more international competition as companies needed to have a larger market base to support their research.
	Prices are constantly being forced down by fierce international competition.
	Technical staff have to be located in the potential sales areas, to sell and then to service.
	Even so, the impact on ICL is probably less than in a consumer goods company since technical companies have for a long time expected to sell some of their output overseas.
Development of the EC	Yes, now that it has overcome the initial antagonism to its Japanese ownership to be accepted as a full member of the European computing community.[11] In 1992 it won important EC research contracts.
State intervention	Yes, both in the ways in which other companies are affected, by taxation and government regulations, and through specific interventions because of governmental interest in having a successful British computer company. The latter included encouragement of the merger between ICT and English Electric in 1968, guaranteeing a large bank loan in 1980, and influencing top management appointments.
Rapid technical change	Yes, the rapidity and costliness of technical change in this industry was the main reason for the early mergers. It remains a dominant feature of the industry.
Social changes	Yes, as in other companies.
Consumerism	Yes, in that it now supplies a consumer as well as a company market.

Table 10.3 *Organizational Changes Affecting ICL*

Organizational changes	Affected ICL or earlier, its constituent companies
Increasing size	Yes, in the early years primarily as a result of the mergers, then a decrease in the number of employees and in the early 1990s a small increase because of acquisitions.
Shrinking organization	Yes, the number of employees dropped from 33,000 in 1980 to 22,000 in 1984, and after the takeover by STC there were further redundancies. More recently the company has also expanded by acquisition and by late 1992 numbers were back over 22,000.
International corporation	Yes, in order to compete successfully ICL has had overseas subsidiaries for many years. The takeover by Fujitsu made it part of a global company in which it also does its own acquisitions.
More fluid boundaries	Yes, though probably less change than many other organizations because many external contacts were always necessary in this dynamic industry.
Change in the staff composition	Yes, the company increasingly needs well qualified people as manufacturing declines and software become more important. It is also affected by the rise in the number of women working and by the attractions for some of them of part-time work.
Changing career patterns	Probably less than in other industries because IT is a very mobile industry.

Table 10.4   *External Changes Affecting the Hospital*

External changes	Affected the general hospital?
One world	Yes, through the large number of foreign staff now employed and their short periods of service with hospitals in the United Kingdom.
EC	No radical impact, but will increasingly affect it; e.g., through common recognition of EC qualifications and the need to observe EC policies in health and safety.
State intervention	Yes, most markedly by establishing the National Health Service with resulting changes in the ownership and organization of hospitals. The intervention has continued in a number of major reorganizations and instructions from the Department of Health. The major reorganization of the NHS from 1990 led to the establishment of Trust hospitals which had greater autonomy and were also exposed to the threats and opportunities of limited competition.
Rapid technical change	Yes, primarily through medical advances and the development of new equipment. These are a major factor, most recently by making day surgery possible for many of the less serious operations and so reducing the number of beds needed. Information technology is, as in other organizations, a potentially major change affecting the nature and organization of some of the work.
Social changes	Yes, especially the higher proportion of patients with different ethnic backgrounds and the need to cater for their distinctive needs. The emphasis on equal career opportunities: 1992 was the start of a drive to increase the number of women in senior posts.
Consumerism	Yes, the introduction of the Patients' Charter in 1992 setting out standards and emphasizing the need to take account of local views of health service needs. Generally, more-vocal clients.

Table 10.5 *Organizational Changes Affecting the Hospital?*

Organizational changes	Affected the general hospital?
Increasing size	Yes, through the establishment of the large district general hospitals, and the closure of smaller hospitals.
Shrinking organization	Yes, by contracting-out services such as laundry and catering and the move to more community-based care.
International corporation	Not applicable.
More fluid boundaries	Yes, primarily as a result of the reorganization of the NHS in which hospitals became dependent upon the purchasing agencies and general practitioner fundholders. Internally, the need to remain viable in a competitive world helped to reduce barriers between departments.
Change in staff composition	Yes, through compulsory tendering of services and the larger number of part-time staff. The reorganization from 1990 on brought more financial and IT staff.
Changing career patterns	The mid-1980s reorganization introduced general managers' posts as a new career option. The later reorganization affected many managerial careers. Less security for hospital consultants is also a likely effect. Nurses' training and careers have had several major changes.

SUMMARY

The chapter has sought to trace the changes in the environment that have affected organizations. Companies are affected by the development of a world economy and a world market-place. All organizations are affected by the development of the EC, state intervention, rapid technical change, social change and the rise of consumerism.

The impact of these changes upon the nature of organizations was summarized in Table 10.1. It suggests that rapid technical change and the growth of one world have had the most varied repercussions.

The increasing size of some organizations was stimulated by state intervention, by rapid technical change and by the opportunities of worldwide markets. The shrinking of many large organizations was caused by recession, competition from other countries, automation, including information technology, and the contracting-out of services. International corporations developed to cater for international markets and to meet competition. One of the most striking changes in organizations is the extent to which boundaries between departments and with the outside world have become more fluid as a result of external pressures. The composition of an organization's employees changed. There are more knowledge workers and fewer people in manual and junior clerical grades. There are many more women workers and many of these work part-time. Job insecurity has increased so many employees are necessarily more mobile. Managers and professional staff move more often between organizations and between employment and self-employment.

These changes were illustrated by what has happened to two types of organization, an IT company, (ICL), and a general hospital.

NOTES

1. D. J. Hickson and C. J. McMillan (eds), *Organization and Nation: The Aston Programme IV* (Aldershot, Hants: Gower, 1981).
2. Hewlett–Packard, *Statement of Corporate Objectives* (Palo Alto, Calif.: Hewlett–Packard, May 1979).
3. Christopher Lorenz, 'When Head Office Goes Native', *Financial Times*, 2 Dec. 1992, p. 18.
4. Angus Foster, 'Stirring up the Waters', *Financial Times*, 15 Jan. 1993, p. 9.
5. Bo L. T. Hedberg, Paul C. Nystrom and William Starbuck, 'Camping on Seesaws: Prescriptions for a Self-designing Organization', *Administrative Science Quarterly*, vol. 21, no. 1 (March 1976) pp. 41–65.
6. Mats Forsgren and Jan Johanson, 'Managing Internationalization in Business Networks', in Mats Forsgren and Jan Johanson (eds), *Managing Networks in International Business* (Philadelphia: Gordon & Breach, 1992) p. 1.
7. A fuller discussion, which includes figures, is given in Rosemary Stewart, *Managing Today and Tomorrow* (London: Macmillan, 1991) pp. 172–5.
8. Fujitsu, *Annual Report, 1991* (Tokyo: Fujitsu, 1992), p. 4.
9. Michael Porter, *The Competitive Advantage of Nations* (New York: Free Press, 1990).
10. Martin Campbell-Kelly, *ICL: A Business and Technical History* (Oxford: Clarendon Press, 1990).
11. Alan Cane, 'Japanese-owned ICL Wins Brussels Research Contracts', *Financial Times*, 1 Sept. 1992.

11 Changing the Organization

The top management of many organizations in Britain and in other countries are trying to make major changes. In companies it is usually competitive pressure that provides the spur to do so; in the Civil Service, local authorities and the National Health Service it is government pressure now partially supplemented by competition. This chapter describes the kind of changes that are most often wanted and the lessons that can be learnt from examples of successful change. An alternative title could be 'Changing the Culture', for that is how many managers describe their aim in organizational change. The broader title is used because cultural change is only one aspect of successful organizational change.

In the last chapter, 'The Changing Organization', we saw that organizations are now more vulnerable to outside pressures, whether they come from competitors, from customers, from politicians or from community pressure groups. We saw, too, that changes in the world economy and in the rapidity of technical change require that companies respond faster than before to changes that affect their profitability. This increased vulnerability means that many organizations need to change in four ways:

1. in their ability to anticipate potential external threats to the organization;
2. in their ability to try to prevent or modify adverse effects;
3. in the speed of their response to adverse changes in their environment;
4. in their ability to make use of the opportunities provided by change.

WHAT KIND OF CHANGES?

A major change in any organization means making a variety of different kinds of change. It always involves modifying the structure, but this is useless unless it is accompanied by changes in what people do, and what people do will not alter sufficiently unless their attitudes to their work change too.

The exact nature of the changes that are wanted will obviously vary with the kind of organization. In the public services the emphasis is on pushing down decision-making and ensuring that accountability is clearly defined. In many companies there is a similar aim which underlies the move to divi-

149

sionalization. A common aim is to create semi-autonomous accountable units whose performance is measurable, whether they are subsidiary companies, individual works, branches, areas or hospitals. In some organizations the performance criteria are clear, in others the search is on for the right performance measures. It is often harder to find satisfactory performance measures in the public sector.

Another common change aim, especially for service organizations whether public or private, is to make employees more customer conscious. This was one of the qualities highlighted in the bestseller, *In Search of Excellence*, reporting on the lessons from America's best-run companies.[1] In the chapter ' Close to the Customer', Peters and Waterman highlighted an obsession with service and quality as characteristics of successful companies. Simple prescriptions, such as their eight conditions for excellence, have great appeal. Doubts arose about whether the eight really are the keys to success when some of the 'excellent' companies later did badly. Geert Hofstede, the Dutch anthropologist, argues that Peters and Waterman's suggestion that there is 'one best way' to organizational excellence, with one set of desirable organizational cultural characteristics, is wrong. His criticisms are based on a comparative study of organizational cultures. The study, directed by Hofstede, from 1985 to 1987, was of 20 organizational units from ten different organizations, half in Denmark and half in Holland. The organizations were in manufacturing and service companies and in the public sector. The study used both in-depth interviews and comparative questionnaires. Hofstede suggests that the culture of these organizations could be compared on six different dimensions. His most important conclusion for those concerned with organizational change was that:

> What is good or bad depends in each case on where one wants the organization to go, and a cultural feature that is an asset for one purpose is unavoidably a liability for another . . . In particular the popular stress on customer orientation . . . is highly relevant for organizations engaged in services and the manufacturing of custom-made quality products, but may be unnecessary or even harmful for, for example, the manufacturing of standard products in a competitive price market.[2]

LESSONS FROM SUCCESSFUL CHANGE

General lessons can be drawn from successful changes in very different kinds of organization. Some apply to any attempts to make major changes in an organization, others are only relevant to particular kinds of change.

These lessons show both the steps that are often necessary to achieve successful change and some of the methods of doing so.

Identifying the Vision

In the past managers talked about goals and objectives. For some years now it has been fashionable to talk first about the vision. This is because so many organizations are having to change radically rather than incrementally. Where change is radical, leaders have to build a bridge between the present and the future if people are to understand and be committed to what is happening. Articulating a vision, that is a credible and attractive future for the organization, is a way of doing that.

Defining What is Wrong

In many organizations, doing this will start with a strategic analysis that identifies the organization's distinctive strengths and weaknesses, the threats that face it and the opportunities that exist. Conducting such an analysis requires an ability to face reality, to recognize the threats to and the weaknesses of the organization, and an understanding of its culture. The culture of an organization is most easily recognized either by comparing it with another organization or with the help of outsiders. It is salutary to start with a study of what actually happens, of how customers or clients are treated, followed by a survey of staff attitudes and of the reasons for them.

Analysis of what is wrong will usually include, even if it does not start with, a review of how the organization is working. Most change plans will focus on changes to the organization. The changes made in 1991 by Hewlett Packard, the American computer company, is one such example. The company's founders Bill Hewlett and David Packard came out of retirement to devise a new organization to meet current needs. David Packard described the problem, in terms that would appeal to those who remember the classical writers on management:

> There has been a build-up of unnecessary bureaucracy in the company ... a lot of emphasis on a matrix management structure in which responsibility and authority is so confused you don't know who the hell is responsible for what.[3]

The new structure pushed decision-making downwards – as is common in many reorganizations today – and split the company into just two product groups to eliminate some of the boundary problems that had arisen in the previous three-group division.

Kent County Council is an early example of a local authority which also pushed decision-making downwards. A new chief executive gave responsibilities for the Council's services, such as libraries and home helps, to the people who delivered them. Departments became business units headed by business managers who could buy in the services they needed. Paul Sabin, the chief executive, applied three principles to guide the reorganization: getting closer to the customer; devolving responsibility; and management not administration.[4] Similar kinds of changes are now being made throughout much of the public sector.

Deciding What to Do

Many action plans start from the need to respond to a new situation. Often for companies the new situation involves a change in the market, for public services from a government-imposed reorganization or from a change in the amount of money available. A good example of an external change requiring companies to make major changes was the institution of new rules governing the operation of financial companies in Britain. Clearing banks, building societies, stockbrokers, jobbers and others had to decide how to respond to a new situation which opened up competition between different kinds of financial companies. For example, the profits of British clearing banks were threatened by competition from building societies, foreign banks and other financial institutions. Another threat to them came from developments in information technology which enabled their customers, particularly their large corporate customers, to make much better use of their own money, and even to act as their own bankers.

The challenge to the banks was to decide what services they could offer to their customers that would enable the banks to retain their profitability. The technical revolution in the handling of money arising from information technology meant that information about money has become almost as important as money itself. This information is one of the services that banks and other financial institutions are selling.

This dual revolution affecting financial institutions in Britain has forced affected companies to think about the changes that they should make over a very broad front. The need for a major review of strategy has been an obvious necessity – changes are needed in the services that should be offered. One response is to become a financial service institution offering a wide range of services rather than specializing in a particular service like banking or life insurance. This has been achieved by mergers, acquisitions, joint ventures and buying a partial interest in a different kind of financial institution. Another response is to change the ways in which existing services are offered; home banking via the television screen is one such example. Greater competitive pressure means productivity must be improved and customers wooed and retained. For such financial companies the comfortable days have gone, as they have for many other companies in Britain and elsewhere. The changes also provide opportunities for new businesses. One example is the 24-hour telephone banking service available throughout the year from First Direct, which showed that the demand for such a service existed every day, even including Christmas day.

The comfortable days have gone in other kinds of organization as well. The cuts in public money to many government-funded organizations have led to economies and staff reductions. An additional or alternative response has been to find other sources of money. An outstanding example in the early 1980s was Salford University, which suffered an unusually severe 40 per cent cut in its income from the University Grants Commission (the arms-length body at that time for distributing government money to British universities). Three years later a new vice-chancellor had helped the staff to earn their way out of this problem by selling research consultancy, by developing a screening service for heart disease and by attracting foreign students to special programmes such as diplomatic studies for Middle Eastern students. This change was inevitably criticized, one academic being quoted as saying, 'We're very close to the point that we're generating so much money from outside that we're no longer a university in the accepted sense'.[5] However, for many organizations, accepted notions about what they are and do will have to change if the organizations are to survive.

Decisions about what changes are needed may require a review of strategy. For a company this may lead to a redefinition of what business it is in. In the public sector, too, as in the Salford University example, it can lead to changes in the products that it is offering to the market-place. 'Products' and 'market-place' are new words for those who work in the public sector. Even hospital consultants working in the new trust hospitals have to take account of what services the purchasing authorities and the GP fundholders are willing to buy from them.

Making change decisions requires more specific analysis and goal- and target-setting than in the past. This is commonplace in companies now, but it is also part of the discipline imposed upon many parts of the public sector, though the penalties for failure may be less harsh.[6]

Common, too, in organizations in the public and private sectors in the early 1990s is the emphasis on improving quality. BS 5750, the set of disciplines for which this publicly certified standard can be awarded, is the method increasingly chosen to seek to ensure that standards for quality are reality, not just rhetoric. The chief executive of a company with many different service sites described its value:

> BS 5750 is the logical conclusion to our development programme in a service based industry where the services we provide have to work first time, every time. This is a zero defects policy. The idea is to provide a consistently high level of service across the country. That zero defects is a minimum standard not a target to be striven for is a powerful concept.
>
> Implementing BS 5750 has been enormously helpful in that it has brought together, in a structured and disciplined manner, a tightening up of operations, procedures and standards. Having listened to a lot of people who have done it before, and spoken to consultants and read countless volumes, the key to quality improvement appears to be to keep it simple. If it is kept commensensical then it seems to work admirably.

Whatever the stimulus for change, plans for what should be done must be closely linked to their implementation. This means being aware of the possible obstacles to change and seeking ways of overcoming them. Usually it is wise to involve in the planning those who must implement any change – 'usually' because there may be circumstances when this cannot be done because of the need for secrecy or because individuals would not agree to changes that affect them adversely.

Gaining Acceptance

A general guide is that people will support what they help to create. However, some changes can only be seen in negative terms by the affected individuals. In such cases the reasons for such painful changes, perhaps involving loss of jobs, skills or status, should be explained. This cannot be done effectively by impersonal communication; managers must personally explain and seek to obtain commitment to the changes. Trevor Owen, for example, when managing director of Remploy, the government company that employs disabled people, personally visited each of the 94 factories in the first year he was in the job and continued to visit each one every two years, spending two days at each factory and meeting every employee. Such personal communication made it easier to get acceptance for the need to change the products that some of the factories produced. He used a variety of other ways of communicating with and consulting managerial staff, including formal meetings with small groups on a regular rota, and also gave an annual personal financial report to employees.

A chief executive who is trying to turn round an organization may need to do a lot of personnel development if he or she is to be successful. Staff who are accustomed to low standards of performance need to learn what high standards are. One chief executive explained how important he thought this was:

> If there is one thing that characterizes my job here, it has been the large element of teaching and coaching. Before you can be a good coach, I think you have to make sure that everybody understands the rules you are trying to play to and why, the dimensions of the field and how you count the goals for and against.
>
> I use sports analogies quite a lot in describing what is required. I find that most people have an interest in a sport and once you know what that is you can normally translate what you are trying to do into suitable language. It also depersonalizes a lot of it. People can readily understand, for example, if it is explained that rather than being a poor opening bat, as a leg spinner, they are a valuable member of the team.

Removing Poor Performers

A frequent action by top managers who take over an organization with problems is to remove those whom they judge to perform badly. They may do this ruthlessly, taking only a short time to make sure that their judgement is correct, and firing the people with only the minimum necessary notice and payments. Alternatively, they may do it as carefully, as kindly and as generously as they can. Either way, they will see it as a necessary step for the health of the organization.

There are a few successful turnround managers who pride themselves on successfully implementing change without getting rid of people. One of these said:

> This is my third turnround situation. With one or two exceptions, I have never got rid of managers. I believe when I get to that stage it is a failure on my part as well as theirs. I just move managers about and get the team together. That is what I can contribute, I think.

Changing the Culture

The word 'culture' is now a popular one, although many people who use it may find it difficult to define what they mean. A simple description is: 'The customary ways of thinking and behaving'. A more elaborate and careful definition can help to give a better understanding of what is meant by the word, such an understanding being useful to the manager who wants to change the culture of an organization. Edgar Schein gives such a definition:

> Organizational culture is the pattern of basic assumptions that a given group has invented, discovered or developed in learning to cope with its problems of external adaptation and internal integration, and that have worked well enough to be considered valid, and, therefore, to be taught to new members as the correct way to perceive, think, and feel in relation to those problems.[7]

An important feature of Schein's definition is the emphasis on basic assumptions that are shared by members of a group. He goes on to explain that these assumptions are typically unconscious, but determine 'how group members perceive, think and feel'. Another important aspect of his definition is that these assumptions developed because they helped adaptation to the environment and integration amongst group members.

A change in culture is required when the characteristics of the culture are no longer suited to a changed environment. They may still promote cohesion amongst members of the group, but the external threat to the group's existence may be too great for that to be relevant.

The first task in cultural change is to decide what people need to do differently and what are the attitudes and assumptions that support their present ways of behaving. University teachers in Britain, for example, had long worked on the assumption that the government would continue to provide the money to support their universities and jobs. Their task was with teaching and research, not with enlisting support for what they did nor with discovering what they could offer that other people would pay for. The example given earlier of Salford University showed how staff at one university adapted to a threat to their jobs. The time that many senior academics in the University of Oxford have been spending in support of the University's or their college's appeal is another, though more minor, example. Another example of how professionals may respond to a threat to their jobs or to their goals can be seen in the willingness of some doctors to get involved in hospital management.

A picture of the changes that are wanted in people's attitudes and behaviour can be built up by asking for words that describe the present culture and the culture that is desired. For example, a group of the district general managers in the National Health Service, who were appointed to help to produce the changes recommended in the Griffiths Report, gave the list shown in Figure 11.1.

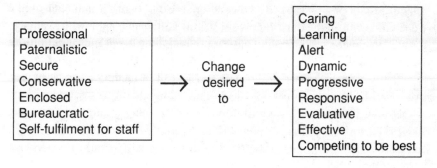

Figure 11.1 *Changes recommended in the NHS culture*

That analysis was made in 1987, but senior managers in the NHS who are trying to implement the latest reorganization would be likely to give a similar list of the desired culture. The description of the aspects of the present culture which they wished to change would show some changes. The deletions are likely to be: Paternalistic, Secure and Enclosed. This suggests that the reorganizations have made the culture of the NHS less secure and inward-looking but that much still needs to be done.

Changing organizational culture in any large organization is a difficult and lengthy task which may well not be successful. Some query whether it is possible, but there are some success stories that suggest it can be done.

There is a danger of getting too attracted by the idea of organizational culture. It has become, as Hofstede has pointed out, a fad, although he does suggest some steps for trying to change the culture.[8] This fad is one of many examples of senior managers being attracted by a new prescription for coping with organizational problems. Like its predecessors the potential for change is overrated and the difficulty of doing so is underrated.

It may be easy to decide what needs to be done differently, but much harder to get this accepted, particularly where there is no external threat to survival. Sometimes, instead of the slow and hard process of trying to change the culture of an existing organization, an easier and faster way may be to set up a new organization as a separate division or subsidiary company, protected from interference by the parent. This option is more often available in companies than in public-sector organizations.

THE CONTRIBUTION OF CHANGE AGENTS

Change agents try to help others to change successfully. What they do is called 'organization development' or OD. A change agent may be an external consultant or a member of the personnel department. Where change has to be made within the existing organization, a change agent may be of help, particularly when top management cannot make sufficient time available or lacks the skill to communicate successfully the need for change. Even where top management is interested and skilful, a change agent may still give useful advice as an outsider with a different perspective.

OD is a philosophy, a way of approaching problems and a set of techniques. Part of the philosophy is a belief in a healthy organization characterized by open communication, mutual trust and confidence between and across levels. Some of the techniques are quite simple, like the mirror image, where two antagonistic groups are asked to role-play each other's group and to describe how they see their own group. The simpler techniques can be used by managers themselves, but they need to be aware of the assumptions they are making in using them.

Individual change agents may differ in their approach and in the techniques they use. Those who are trained in psychoanalysis, for example, will lay stress upon the importance of unconscious processes in affecting how people behave. Some may still favour techniques like the T group, which uses group reactions to help individuals get a better understanding of how they appear to other people. Others may think such techniques too dangerous. Despite these differences, change agents do share some common assumptions and ways of approaching problems.

One of the starting points for change agents is that the conventional analysis of problems is not adequate for identifying either what the real problems are or how they should be tackled. Another is that any major change involves not only learning something new but also unlearning something that is currently accepted as part of the culture and which is one of the very reasons for resistance to change. Further, there must be a motivation to change if change is to take place. One of the ideas used by OD consultants is that of the need for 'unfreezing' before change can occur. Therefore, change is most readily accepted where the need for it is clear, as it was in wartime or as it is in any situation where there is an external threat to the existing way of life. Where there is no such generally recognized threat, getting acceptance that change is necessary can be one of the hardest tasks in trying to effect organizational change.

The next stage in the change process, after unfreezing, is the development of new attitudes and behaviours. The final stage is called 're-freezing', that is stabilizing the changes so that people do not slip back into their old ways of thinking and behaving.

The change agent has three potential advantages. One is being an outsider – an advantage not held by internal change agents unless they are working in a different and unfamiliar part of the organization. An outsider can notice aspects of the culture that are so familiar to its members that they may not be aware of them. The second advantage of the change agent is that she or he has time and is there specifically to facilitate change; managers trying to carry through similar changes have, in addition, their normal work to undertake. The third advantage is that of knowledge and experience – knowledge of the process of change and of the problems that are likely, and experience of helping others to manage it. These advantages mean that change agents can help. Managers can and often do carry through changes successfully without them, but it takes time, understanding and sensitivity to do so – time spent in discussions with others, both in identifying what needs to be done and in helping to get that accepted, understanding of the reasons for other people's reactions, and sensitivity to be aware of the reactions.

ORGANIZATIONAL LEARNING

The phrase 'organizational learning' started to be used in the 1980s to describe what was required if organizations were to adapt successfully to their changing environments – to learn faster than their competitors. It was a theme of Richard Pascale's fascinating book, *Managing on the Edge*, which discussed the problems that companies had in staying successful. He quotes with approval one Ford executive who said: 'MBOs are not helpful. We do not want static objectives. We want a process that is obsessed with constantly improving things.'[9] Pascale says that it is essential for organizations to do two types of learning: little learning, which is incremental improvement; and big learning, which is shifting the context of the base line. It is the habit of inquiry that makes for learning. Describing three outstanding chief executives he says:

> Each problem they solved created the opportunity to solve the next problem that their last solution created. They displayed the characteristic of not just 'having the answers' but of 'living-in-the question'. They ask questions not merely to generate *answers* but to reveal *what is possible*.[10]

Peter Senge in *The Fifth Discipline* devotes a whole book to 'The Art and Practice of the Learning Organization' in which he tries to describe what a learning organization would be like.[11] He identifies four core disciplines for building a learning organization. The first is through individual learning, which he calls 'personal mastery' in its broadest sense of personal growth. The second is developing and being able to articulate mental models for discussing management. The third is a shared vision, and the fourth is team learning which requires a shared language for dealing with complexity. These all require his fifth discipline, which is systems thinking, that is the ability to see interrelationships.

Earlier we quoted Hofstede saying that organizational culture is a fad. Organizational learning is not, at least yet, a fad. Fads fade because there is a reaction to their excesses. It is a pity when a potentially useful contribution to our thinking about organizations seems likely to fade because it has become a fad; it is to be hoped that will not happen to organizational learning.

Most readers are unlikely to be in a position to exercise the amount of influence that is required to try to effect major changes in organizational culture, including its ability to learn. However, all, except the most adept, can improve their ability to question as well as to listen and to consider what others say.

COMMON FAILURES

The fourth annual survey, *Commitment: Implementing the Vision*, by Ingersoll Engineers, a UK consultancy, identified some common failings in implementing change amongst 200 senior executives of manufacturing companies. The main failures that they found were in not giving enough priority to detailed planning and implementation or to communicating adequately, especially to supervisors who will have to implement the changes.[12]

The language used by Ingersoll Engineers for describing failures is different from that of writers on organizational learning. In reading about the management of change it is worth asking 'How does the writer view that task?', which is another way of asking 'What mental model is being used?' Ingersoll Engineers describe the failures in language that derive from the classical school of management. Writers on transformational leadership and on organizational learning are trying to change the way people see the world. Both views of organizational change are useful to the management of change: neither is sufficient in itself. The danger is in thinking that they are.

SUMMARY

Many managers in Britain and other countries are trying to make major changes. These changes are of a similar nature in different kinds of organization, so managers have a wide variety of examples of successful change upon which to draw in order to encourage and help them in their own efforts. Any major change requires a variety of different kinds of change – changes in structure, in what people do and in their attitudes to what needs to be done. A review of strategy will be required if there is an external threat to the organization. The products or services that are being provided and the ways that this is done may, as in banking, require radical change. Frequent aims of change are increased productivity, improved quality, better service to customers and a greater desire to serve customers well.

The process of change is complex because of the variety of changes that may be necessary and the different stages in the process. Examples of successful change can be studied for the lessons that they can provide at each stage. The first step may be to define what is wrong. This is often difficult because it is hard to face up to reality if it is unpleasant. The next stage, which can also be the first step when there is a clear external threat, is to decide what to do. This may need a major review of strategy as well as detailed planning. Examples are given of how organizations changed their activities to meet an external threat.

Plans for change must be closely linked to implementation. The possible obstacles to change should be recognized. Gaining acceptance of the need for change may be the hardest task where there is no obvious external threat to the organization. Those who will have to implement any change should, as far as practical, be involved in planning the change; this will make acceptance easier. Explaining the need for change is time consuming. It is best done by the boss talking directly to those affected.

Many major changes require a cultural change before new ways of thinking and acting can take root. It helps both to understand the attitudes and assumptions that support present behaviour and to provide support and rewards for change. Where it is very hard to change attitudes, it may be easier, where it is practical, to set up a separate organization protected from interference from the parent.

Change agents are people who specialize in helping organizations to change. Another name for them is organization development (OD) consultants. OD is a philosophy, a way of approaching problems and a set of techniques. Change agents start with the need for unfreezing current attitudes, then go on to help people to change before finally establishing new attitudes and behaviour. Managers can manage change successfully, without the help of change agents, but such agents can be of help in understanding what is happening during the change and thus in reducing some of the obstacles to it.

The need for organizational learning is the latest addition to accounts of change management. Organizations are having to adapt to external changes much more often and much faster than in the past. This means that their employees have to be able to learn and to continue learning. Organizational change is no longer a number of sporadic one-offs: it is an on-going process which requires a spirit of inquiry for successful adaptation.

NOTES

1. Thomas J. Peters and Robert H. Waterman, *In Search of Excellence: Lessons from America's Best Run Companies* (New York: Harper & Row, 1982).
2. Geert Hofstede, *Cultures and Organizations: Software of the Mind* (London: McGraw-Hill, 1991) p. 199.
3. Louise Kehoe, 'A Reserved Player Comes Out Fighting', *Financial Times*, 22 March 1991.
4. Sarah Hegarty, 'An Entrepreneur at the Council', *Independent*, 4 June 1992.
5. *The Economist*, 16 Feb. 1985, pp. 25–6.
6. Colin Duncan (ed.), *The Evolution of Public Management: Concepts and Techniques for the 1990s* (London: Macmillan, 1992) is one of several books providing the new techniques for the public sector.
7. Edgar H. Schein, 'Coming to a New Awareness of Organizational Culture', *Sloan Management Review*, Winter 1984.
8. Hofstede, *Cultures and Organizations*, p. 202.
9. Richard Tanner Pascale, *Managing on the Edge: How Successful Companies Use Conflict to Stay Ahead* (London: Viking, 1990) p. 173.
10. Ibid., p. 262.
11. Peter M. Senge, *The Fifth Discipline: The Art and Practice of the Learning Organization* (New York: Doubleday Currency, 1990).
12. Ingersoll Engineers, *Commitment: Implementing the Vision* (Bourton Hall, Rugby, Warks.: Ingersoll Engineers, 1992).

12 Providing Managers for Changing Organizations

Organizations need competent managers who can successfully run existing activities. They need managers who can avoid or cope with the threats that face most companies and, increasingly, public-sector organizations as well. They need, too, managers who can make good use of available opportunities. There should be an adequate supply of suitable managers to fill vacancies as they arise, except where they can be obtained from outside.

Many of the problems of providing the managers required are similar to those of the past, so we shall start by looking at them. The supply of good managers is somewhat easier than before because greater managerial mobility and more management education has provided a better pool of qualified talent on which to draw. Organizations make greater use of search consultants as they no longer think they must find managers only from inside. The changes affecting organizations discussed in Chapter 10 have also brought new problems in providing a supply of competent managers. These will be described in the second part of the chapter.

WHAT REMAINS THE SAME

Management succession must take place in all organizations, even the more stable ones, simply because managers are promoted, leave, retire or die. In some organizations management succession is unplanned, but where management is striving to be efficient it is seen as an important part of organizational planning.

The term 'manager' is used here in the broadest sense, describing all those above the level of supervisors who are responsible for the activities of other people or who perform a specialist role without subordinates that contributes to management. This excludes those doing a purely professional job, such as design engineer, research chemist and physiotherapist,[1] but includes those who may be moved to a specialist job after holding an operational management job. In some organizations such moves are a part of career development.

Major problems of management succession are as follows:

163

1. to determine the numbers and types of managers likely to be needed in the future;
2. to decide what kinds of career patterns are desirable. This is such a large problem that it can be subdivided as follows:
   - What is the catchment group for potential managers? This is another way of asking where the management career ladder should start. If university graduates are considered the main source of future managers, what provision should be made for other types of entrants to gain access to the management ladder?
   - Should later entrants be part of the plan for management succession or merely a resource when there are no suitable internal candidates?
   - Should a manager's career begin with experience in a technical or professional post or with a more general training in the organization's activities?
   - What form of transfers or promotions between different parts of the organization are desirable and practicable?
   - How can able managers be given the kind of experience that will help to equip them to fill more senior posts successfully?
   - Is it desirable to appoint people to top management posts when they are in their thirties or early forties?
3. to decide when organizational requirements are more important than individual needs, and vice versa;
4. to retain and motivate ambitious and able men and women, especially when the organization is not expanding.

This list does not include many of the more technical problems that must be considered in trying to provide for future management such as: how to select the most suitable candidates for a position; how to assess potential; what kind of training to provide, and so on. The main focus here is on the nature of managerial careers and on management succession rather than on methods of management development.

DETERMINING FUTURE MANAGEMENT NEEDS

In the foreseeable future, how many and what kinds of managers are likely to be needed? This is a question that should be considered in any continuing organization. Is the organization likely to expand, to remain the same size or to contract? Can any estimate be made of the likely size of the expansion or contraction? Management may say that it is impossible to predict, or even to try to estimate, what the likely size and shape of the organization will be in five years' time, far less in 20 years' time, yet the recruitment of potential managers will be based on some assumptions about this, even if these are not made explicit. The larger the organization the more true this will be, merely because of the numbers involved. However, the rapid changes affecting organizations make it even harder than in the past to determine future management needs.

It is even more difficult to decide what assumptions should be made about the future composition of management. Is it reasonable to assume that the organization is likely to remain the same shape, so that the same proportions of managers as before are needed at each level of management? The traditional management hierarchy is pyramid-shaped, so that many more junior managers are needed than middle managers, and far fewer top managers than middle managers. This traditional shape has changed in many organizations, as we saw in an earlier chapter, because of changes in the composition of the staff and concomitant changes in the numbers and kinds of managers required at different levels. The importance of different management tasks has also altered to cope with a changing environment. Ansoff points out the growth in the importance of general, compared with functional, management. He attributes this to the need to ensure the development of strategies to respond to external changes.[2] Since he wrote in 1984, the number of general managers relative to functional managers has increased further. This is because of decentralization to accountable units headed by a general manager.

The decline in large-scale manufacturing and the growth of new smaller-scale research-based industries such as electronics and biotechnology has reduced the need for production managers and increased that for development staffs. For example, in one division of a major electronics firm there are two employees in product development for each one in assembly. Rapid product change means that there must also be more people in marketing.

Changes in the technical and professional composition of management provide another tricky problem for management-succession planning. Even if a company gets its estimates of numbers right, it may still be badly wrong about the type of people who are required. The problem of getting the right mix of professional and technical skills is much greater in an organization that needs many managers with this kind of background than it is for a commercial or administrative organization, where most recruits can be of undifferentiated management potential. How much of a problem this is will also depend upon the career policies in the organization and whether they promote within specialities or aim to produce managers with more general skills by transfers across departments. The right mix is usually thought of in terms of technical and professional qualifications, but the right mix of abilities can also be important. It is unusual for organizations to attempt to recruit for different levels of managerial potential. Most set a minimum level of academic attainment and above that select the best candidates they can get, instead of deliberately aiming at a range of abilities. This probably remains as true today as when McClelland said in 1968: 'This situation can be tolerated only so long as the predictive value of selection procedures remains so low.'[3] He pointed out that in the absence of a rapid turnover there are large differences in the ultimate extent of promotion of entrants selected on similar criteria.

CAREER PATTERNS FOR MANAGEMENT

Planning career patterns for different types of entrants is part of a policy for management succession, as well as providing evidence that the company has a career policy. There is still, even in times of recession, competition for the best graduates, who expect to know what their career prospects are likely to be, at least in the short term. They will rarely be satisfied with general comments such as 'unlimited scope' or 'the future is up to you', and very sensibly too – it is very easy to get overlooked in a large organization. One must be promoted sufficiently rapidly in the early years to be in the running for top jobs later. In large organizations there should therefore be a system for checking on how career planning is working out in practice. Computerized personnel records make this much easier than in the past. They can provide the answers to questions about the kinds of job experience that present managers have had, and this can then be compared against current views of what experience is needed for top management.

Where should the management career ladder start? The traditional answer used to be 'At the bottom – come in on the shopfloor or in the office and work your way up to the top.' In large organizations this is rare today, and is likely to become rarer still. Most such organizations are now looking to the university graduate and the later school-leaver for their potential managers, so this is where the management ladder tends to start. There may still be bridges provided from the non-managerial career ladders, but in a large organization there may still be too many rungs to be climbed to give those who start in the lowest-paid jobs much chance of reaching the top. The existence of professional and technical requirements for management posts is also an important limitation to promotion from the bottom; for example, hospital domestic staff cannot rise to become chief nurse, nor is the laboratory assistant likely to be able to qualify by spare-time study for the position of chief chemist in a large company. A still greater barrier than lack of formal qualifications, however, is the time needed to climb up a long ladder when others have started higher up. In many large organizations the ladder is now shorter because some levels of management have been removed, but it remains very hard in most organizations to rise from the bottom to top management. It is somewhat easier in Britain than in Germany. In few British companies would possession of a doctorate be seen to be a good qualification for top management whereas in Germany a recent study showed that a quarter of top managers had doctorates.[4]

The policy of most large organizations used to be to recruit their potential managers at a young age, usually under 25, and to aim to give them a life-long career. The stability, or more usually the growth, assumptions implicit in such a policy are now less likely to come true. Even companies who have been successful for many years may go through a period of difficulty and retrenchment, as many of Peters and Waterman's 'excellent companies' subsequently did. The response to such uncertainties is to become more flexible in providing for management succession. This flexibility includes making early retirement and voluntary redundancies attractive when retrenchment is necessary, even if compulsory redundancies can be avoided. When there are unfilled vacancies organizations may recruit more managers and professionals externally and use people on short-term contracts and on a fee for service. Nowadays there may even be a preference for external recruitment as a way of bringing in new experience and new attitudes and thus making it easier to change the culture. The search for external managerial candidates has been a feature of parts of the public sector which have been forced to become more managerial and more commercial in outlook.

There are two arguments in favour of some older recruits. One is that they can bring new ideas from their experience in other organizations. The other is that they can be a source of able managers rather than just of potential managers, as are the younger entrants. The arguments against a policy of later recruitment are that it reduces promotion opportunities for existing staff and that the newcomers may find it hard to adjust to the culture of the organization. The rapid turnover of general managers recruited from outside the NHS was one example of the problems of adapting to a new culture and of being accepted by it.

There is a sharp policy division between those who believe in recruiting potential managers direct into a specific job, and those who think that they should first be shown something of the range of the organization's activities. Both policies have their advantages and disadvantages. The former has the merit of giving new recruits something that they can do from the beginning and, if they have a relevant qualification, an opportunity to use this. It also means that they can be immediately useful. Against this, it is hard to find something useful to do that is sufficiently demanding for graduates with no specialist qualification. Another disadvantage is that they can rapidly become rather specialized, so that later the organization may have to try and correct the limitations of too narrow an outlook. The disadvantage of the other method – of moving new recruits around – is that they may get bored unless their tour of different departments is well planned and they are given something constructive to do. A further snag is that the new staff are a cost rather than an asset during this time and may leave the organization before they have made any contribution. However, this may well be the easiest time to show them a wide range of the organization's work. It provides an opportunity not only for the new entrants to see which aspect of the organization's work interests them most, but also for different managers to see the new recruits and decide whom they would like to have in their department.

An important and difficult decision that has to be made about career patterns is how narrow or broad they should be in terms of the organization's main activity. The traditional career pattern was for young recruits to go into one department and to be promoted solely within it. This gave them a good knowledge of that department's work and helped to develop strong departmental loyalties. The advantages, however, were also the disadvantages. Those who have spent their whole career in one department are likely to know little of the work of other departments and may find it difficult to understand their problems and point of view. Their dominant loyalty may be to the department rather than to the organization, so that in disputes with other departments they may be likely to put their department's interests first. There is also the important disadvantage that promotion solely within one department is poor preparation for top management, where an appreciation of all aspects of the business is desirable.

The advantages of gaining experience in different parts of the organization are now widely recognized in large British and American companies. In the public sector, too, careers are not quite as functionally dominated as they used to be because of the creation of general management posts at different levels. British and American companies want to provide a varied experience to develop general managers and to help managers adapt to the changing environment. However, in Germany careers are still primarily within the individual functions. The reason is the importance attached to professional and technical expertise rather than to the width of managerial experience. This approach is mirrored in many top management groups which consist of functional heads without a chief executive.

Managers' careers are much more varied than in the past. They move between companies, and to a small extent between public and private sectors, as well as between functions within the same organization. This gives them a better preparation for general management. Radical job moves can help to give managers the greater adaptability they need in rapidly changing organizations, as well as providing the stimulus for rapid personal development, though they do carry the risk of failure and the subsequent blighting of a career.

Transfers between departments are one way of providing wider job experience, although often the most difficult to arrange. Transfers between different locations are another type of job mobility which is used by many large companies that are geographically dispersed. Often, as in branch banking, it may be the main way to get promotion. The value of this kind of mobility is that it can help to prevent too parochial an outlook. Its main disadvantage is its social cost, which fewer managers and their families are now willing to pay.

An aspect of transfers that is often overlooked is the effect that these can have on the pattern of loyalties in the company. Who does the manager think of as 'We'? Is it the department, the division, a subsidiary company, or the company as a whole? Managers who spend a long time in one department or in one local establishment are likely to identify with the department or establishment; indeed, their loyalty to it may be stronger than to the organization as a whole. Career planning should thus take into account the kind of loyalties that managers should be encouraged to develop.

The planning of career patterns should be based on a good understanding of the different types of jobs in the company and of the kind of experience they offer. Such understanding is often all too limited. Most training managers think of jobs as being either junior, middle or top management, and in the more traditional organizations as belonging to one of the main functions, but do not bother to consider other differences. There is too little analysis of the nature of different jobs in the organization and of the ways in which experience in these jobs may help or hinder a manager's development. Wilson pointed out the different skills that may be required at different levels. Skills developed at one level can even be a disqualification for promotion to another where quite different skills are required. Wilson cites the difference between the skills needed at junior levels in financial or commercial departments and those needed in the most senior posts. At the junior levels what is required is patience, accuracy and tolerance of routine. A little higher up, the safeguarding of assets may be an important activity, but at the top, as Wilson says:

The main responsibility is almost the opposite of passive safeguarding of assets; it is that of trying actively to increase the assets by making estimates of probability and by sharing decisions about complex risk-taking, the organized 'gambling', which makes up such an important proportion of top-management work. A man who may well have considerable potential for this high-level work may be seriously handicapped if he spends more than a short period of his career in the routine-dominated lower levels where the primary responsibilities are of a quite different character.[5]

He was writing in the late 1960s but despite the major changes within financial departments his remarks remain true today. However, the risks are less because of the greater job mobility.

There are similar differences in different levels of works management. The more junior and middle levels of production management usually require both good staff management and the ability to deal rapidly with a large number of different queries and minor crises. Jobs are very episodic, and the manager has little opportunity to plan. Too long a time in such a job may make it hard for managers to adjust to the demands of a more senior post where they should devote more time and effort to planning. Similarly, the change from a job that requires managers to respond to others to one where they have to spend more time looking ahead can be difficult. Many works managers may try and evade the problem by spending long hours touring the works. Former bank managers may find the same difficulty when they are promoted to divisional or head office; 'It was dreadful,' said one. 'There I was in a room by myself with lots of papers. Nobody came to see me and the telephone rarely rang.'

It needs to be recognized that some jobs are much better than others for training future top management. The opportunity to practise general man-agement at a young age, in a setting where mistakes will not be too costly, is one valuable form of training. Another is working in a job that brings young managers into close touch with top management. Such a job has the advantage that it enables the occupant of the job to observe something of the nature of top-management work; it also has a more personal advantage, in that it makes him or her visible to top management.

'The average age of our executive directors is 41' – even large organiza-tions may make such a claim. New and smaller ones may boast of even younger top management. In many organizations people are being appointed to top posts at an earlier age than in the past. This, it is urged, helps to keep top management up to date and stops able young managers from being frustrated and from moving to a competitor. This is true, but it can pose severe problems later on. For example, unless the organization is a rapidly expanding one, the top posts may be blocked for 20 years or more, unless, of course, the organization is prepared to bear the costs of early retirement. It can be hard, too, to retain enthusiasm and initiative if one is in the same job for so long. A suggested solution is to switch to a completely different career long before retirement. This is good in theory, perhaps, but there are still not many examples in practice. Meanwhile the problem is likely to become more evident as the present young top managers get older, even though early retirement is much more common than in the past.

Finally, we should remember that promotion is the main way of rewarding exceptional talent, while bearing in mind that this can cause difficulties. For example, it can make it difficult to reward adequately those with exceptional professional skill while letting them continue to practise that skill. There are still complaints about this in some organizations, although a variety of solutions to the problem are now used, such as the long-standing remedy of providing, as ICI does, special status and rewards for outstanding scientists. There is the acceptance, notably in some financial companies, that the chief executive can be paid less than a number of other executives. Sometimes this is the result of taking over another company with a higher salary structure, sometimes it is due to the eagerness of competitors to poach those with financial flair, or it might be the price that must be paid to attract someone with a high reputation from another company. Those who do not want to disturb the salary structure can use external consultants and in that way pay the market rate for specialist knowledge that commands a premium.

BALANCING THE NEEDS OF JOBS AND PEOPLE

All large organizations are to a greater or lesser extent bureaucratic. This means that they consist of posts which continue when their holder leaves, thus making for continuity. In a very bureaucratic organization the job specification, which describes the kind of person who should fill the vacant job, will be precisely laid down, as also may be the categories of employees who are entitled to be considered for the post. The job specification is likely to be more detailed for jobs that have existed for some time than for new jobs where the requirements are not yet as clearly known. In a less bureaucratic organization more attention will be paid to the particular abilities and characteristics of the possible successors and the jobs may be altered to take account of their special strengths or weaknesses. This is most likely to happen in small organizations, where a limited supply of good people may make it imperative to use their abilities to the full.

People vary. Different people, even if they have a similar background, training and ability, may do the same job in different ways. There is – fortunately for us diverse human beings – no one recipe for a good manager. We know that even in highly bureaucratic organizations, such as the armed services, officers can differ in the way they do a particular job. People will adapt the job to some extent to their own interests and abilities, however detailed the job description. Their opportunities for doing so are likely to be greater in the more senior jobs, where the nature of the work can be less clearly defined than in the more junior jobs.

A new managing director may well focus on different aspects of the job from his or her predecessor so that, although the title and the responsibilities remain the same, what is actually done may well be very different. This is most likely where the new MD has a different functional background from the previous one. A change in the work done by a new boss will also have repercussions on the work that needs to be done by immediate subordinates.

The extent to which different people in the same job may spend their time in very different ways was shown in the author's comparisons of the behaviour of managers in similar jobs.[6] These studies highlighted the considerable opportunities for managers, especially senior managers, to choose which aspects of the job to emphasize and which to minimize or ignore. Different managers will notice different things that need doing; their perceptions and their priorities will differ. The study also showed that such choices may not be, and often are not, made consciously.

Individuals adapt jobs to suit themselves. Organizations may also modify the structure to suit the abilities of the people available . This is a long-standing practice in many British and American companies. It reflects the importance attached to the individual's personality and managerial record compared with technical qualifications and experience. This contrasts with the approach in German companies where more importance is given to the latter and hence to the individual fitting the job specification.[7]

The development needs of individuals may conflict with the short-term view of organizational efficiency. They may be ready for a change of job but there may be no suitable vacancies. Should they have to wait until vacancies do exist or should the vacancies be created for them? Usually managers have to wait, but some companies say that they create opportunities for specific people considered to be flyers. Another conflict is that between the time people need to gain useful experience in a job and the often longer time that is needed to get over the learning period and to make a useful contribution. The organization's short-term needs will sometimes have to be sacrificed so that a potential top manager can be given the breadth of experience that may be considered essential for top management in that organization.

WHAT IS DIFFERENT?

Contraction has had dramatic effects on career patterns and expectations. Mobility between employers, both voluntary and in response to redundancy, has greatly increased. In 1958 a study of the careers of British managers showed that a third spent all their working life with one firm. This had dropped to 13 per cent in 1976 and by 1983 to less than 10 per cent. The later study showed that women were even more mobile than men. The 1976 survey found that the managers surveyed had changed their employers on average three times; the 1983 survey found that it had risen to 3.4 for men, while for women it was 3.6. [8]

A 1990 survey by the British Institute of Management of 583 of its members focused on more detailed aspects of mobility so that the figures just given cannot be compared with the latest survey. The 1990 survey found that 39 per cent of managers had not changed employer in the last ten years, which means that 61 per cent had. This was only slightly more than an earlier BIM study in 1981. Most of the job moves were within the same industry.[9]

For individuals the main change has been the much greater job insecurity. A lifetime career in the same large organization is now much less common than in the past, even in much of the public sector. In response many managers are seeking to improve their marketability to offset the threat of redundancy or of not having their short-term contract renewed. The numbers in MBA programmes is but one example of this search for marketable qualifications.

The decline in security is partly offset by the rise of other opportunities. There is more scope than before for self-employment, particularly as a management consultant and for creating new businesses – though few survive. There is more scope, too, for moving between the public and private sectors and it is easier to move to other companies at home or abroad.

For companies many of the traditional problems of management succession and career development remain the same, but finding good solutions to them is now even more important as competent managers are part of a company's competitive edge in an increasingly competitive world. The importance of management development is increasingly recognized by large companies and with it the need to take career planning seriously – in some, such as Shell and Unilever, it has been for very many years. This is less true in the public sector, for example chairmen and non-executives who come into the NHS from businesses, where the pool of talent was well nurtured and well indexed on central computerized personnel records, continue to be horrified by how little is done to ensure a pool of known managerial talent.

There are two major additions to the traditional problems of management development. One is the need to encourage continual learning. It is no longer sufficient, for the company that takes management development seriously, just to think of education and training for the key transitions in the managerial career; a spirit of continued learning should also be encouraged. This is embodied in the idea of a learning organization, which was discussed on pp. 159–60. Facilitating such learning is partly a process of stimulating a spirit of inquiry and partly that of reviewing the best learning opportunities available for developing managers. These can include assignment to special projects, secondment to another organization and radical job moves as well as executive programmes.

Developing managers who can work successfully outside their own country is the other major addition to the tasks of management development and management succession. This is not a new concern for long-established international companies, but many more companies, including relatively small ones, need such managers. Even for international companies there are two new aspects to it: one is developing European managers to work within the EC and the other is the development of global management as distinct from international companies run by nationals from their home base. In the past the chosen solution for managing foreign subsidiaries was to recruit good local managers. Now with business strategies increasingly bridging country boundaries managers are needed who can do so too.

It is the British and especially the American top managers who have most reason to be worried about the ability of their own nationals to become truly European or international. One problem is weakness in foreign languages compared to continental Europeans. The other, and related, problem is lack of sufficient sensitivity to how other nationalities think and to the reasons for differences in approach. Many American personnel journals contain articles describing the inadequacies of American management in adapting to a world that works according to different mores. For example, a survey of American practice in their foreign subsidiaries found that nearly all companies used their American performance rating forms with their foreign nationals rather than developing special materials. Some did not even bother to have the forms translated.[10]

There is a current debate about whether a European manager already exists, but more agreement that the breed is needed to run complex cross-border European businesses. One step that is being taken by European industrialists to promote executive mobility is for members of the European Roundtable of Industrialists, an association of about 40 of the largest European companies, to swap managers for short periods.[11] It is easier for managers of one European country to operate successfully in some of the EC countries than in others. The British and the Dutch, for example, have had two large joint companies, Unilever and Shell, for a long time and are nearer to each other in their style of managing than either are to the French. The German have their own distinctive approach, as has been suggested earlier, so do the Southern Europeans, and both differ from Anglo-Dutch. The Anglo-Saxons have the most generalist view of management development, which also exists in some Dutch companies and is developing in Scandinavia.[12]

There are more managers who have experience of working for other nationalities and for companies with a foreign parent so that they learn to cope with these differences. One British manager who had previously worked for an American company and later for a French one commented on one of the differences that he noticed: 'The French do not believe in encouragement. Our year's results were good, but the French seemed more concerned that we had exceeded the targets they had set us than pleased that we had good results.'

SUMMARY

There are three long-standing problems in providing for management succession. The first is determining how many and what kinds of managers will be needed in the future. In a large organization some assumptions about this must be made, either explicitly or implicitly, when recruiting.

The second problem is deciding what kind of career patterns are desirable. This requires decisions to be made about the type of career ladders that should exist. Where should the management ladder start? What provisions can and should be made for those who start on a more junior ladder in order that they can get on to the managerial one? Is it desirable to encourage transfers from one ladder to another? If so, what transfers are practicable and when should they be made? The idea of a career ladder is itself out of date in some organizations, where the extent of job rotation means that separate career ladders do not exist in the same form as they did in the more traditional organization. Should a potential manager's career begin with a general training in the activities of the organization or in a specific post? The advantages and disadvantages of different policies are discussed. It is urged that management development officers should know enough about each kind of job in their organization to understand what type of experience it provides. Some junior and middle management jobs require qualities that are the opposite of those needed in senior posts in the same function.

The third problem lies in deciding when organizational requirements are more important than individual needs, and vice versa. This applies to the need to fill specific jobs compared with the possibility of creating or adapting jobs to suit the strengths and weaknesses of particular individuals. Career planning, particularly for those judged to have high potential, may mean balancing short-term organizational needs against possible long-term advantages.

There are two newer problems in providing for managers who can deal successfully with the changes affecting their organizations. One is that of encouraging continuing learning, so that managers are prepared to respond successfully and even to anticipate the changes. The other is developing managers who can work in other countries and who can manage cross-country alliances.

Individual managers continue to face great career insecurity. To try and counter this threat the prudent ones have sought to ensure their marketability by improving their qualifications and getting varied job experience.

NOTES

1. This definition of 'managers' is based on that in Liam Gordon, Ruth Mandy, Tony Moyniham and Roderick Murphy, *Managers in Ireland* (Dublin: Irish Management Institute, 1974) p. 10.

2. H. Igor Ansoff, *Implanting Strategic Management* (Englewood Cliffs, N.J.: Prentice-Hall, 1984).

3. W. G. McClelland, 'Career Patterns and Organizational Needs', in R. J. Hacon (ed.), *Organizational Necessities and Individual Needs*, ATM Occasional Papers, no. 5 (Oxford: Basil Blackwell, 1968) p. 26.

4. W. Eberwein and J. Tholen, *Management as Function and Profession* (Berlin, London: De Gruyter, 1993).

5. A. T. M. Wilson, 'Some Sociological Aspects of Systematic Management Development', in R. J. Hacon (ed.), *Organizational Necessities and Individual Needs*, ATM Occasional Papers, no. 5 (Oxford: Basil Blackwell, 1968).

6. Rosemary Stewart, *Choices for the Manager* (Maidenhead, Berks.: McGraw-Hill; Englewood Cliffs, N.J. : Prentice-Hall, 1982).

7. This and other remarks about German management in this chapter come from a comparative Anglo-German study of middle managers in which the author took part. It is to be published as *Managing in Britain and Germany*, Rosemary Stewart, Jean-Louis Barsoux, Dieter Ganter, Alfred Kieser and Peter Walgenbach (London: Macmillan, 1994).

8. B. Alban-Metcalfe and N. Nicholson, *The Career Development of British Managers*, BIM Foundation Management Survey Report (London: British Institute of Management, 1984).

9. Trudy Coe and Andrew Stark, *On the Move: Manager Mobility in the 1990s* (Corby, Northants: British Institute of Management, 1991) p. 4.

10. Stephen Hayden, 'Our Foreign Legions are Faltering', *Personnel*, Aug. 1990, p. 41.

11. 'The Elusive Euro-manager', Management Focus, *The Economist*, 7 Nov. 1992, p. 109.

12. Paul Evans, Elizabeth Lank and Alison Farquhar discuss cultural traditions in management development in 'Managing Human Resources in the International Firm: Lessons from Practice', in Paul Evans, Yves Doz and André Laurent (eds), *Human Resource Management in International Firms* (London: Macmillan, 1989) pp. 123–30.

Conclusions – What Can Go Wrong?

Any organization needs to be reviewed periodically to see that it is still appropriate for current needs. This is true both of the organization as a whole and of its individual parts. When doing so it is useful to remember some of the common mistakes that can be made setting up organizations, that can develop with time or that can develop in rapidly changing conditions. This chapter is intended as a brief guide to these mistakes. The questions can be used as a checklist to help expose particular mistakes.

Most of those described below are long-standing mistakes. Some of them are now less common because companies have had to improve the management of their organizations in order to survive. However, they are still worth including because no improvements are permanent and there is always a danger of reverting to previous common mistakes. Some mistakes, such as numbers 3 and 4, have a remarkable longevity.

1. What objectives have been set? Do these cover all the main aspects of the organization?

The need to be clear about one's objectives has become almost a cliché, yet any list of common mistakes must still start with it.

There are two dangers: one is that only lip-service will be paid to the need; the other is that what is meant by objectives can be too general to be a useful guide to planning. In business it is not sufficient to say that one's objective is to make a profit, as that leaves so many questions unanswered. Nor it is sufficient, say, in hospitals to state that one's aim is to care for patients. What is needed is a series of objectives, covering each of the main areas of the organization's activities. In a company these will include, among others, the amount of profit, the level of productivity, the kind of markets that it wants to serve and the standing it is aiming for in those markets. Some of these are now also required in public-sector organizations; others have always been common to business, the public sector and voluntary organizations, such as objectives for the treatment of employees.

Only when management has defined its objectives for the different areas can it decide what is likely to be the best form of organization to meet them. For example, does the company aim to offer after-sales service? If it does, it will need a different form of organization from one that does not do so. Is the aim to expand sales overseas? A company that provides after-sales service will have to think carefully before selling in new areas. It will need to be clear about its marketing policy, including whether the aim is to concentrate on selected markets, before deciding on the most suitable organization to support overseas markets.

- *Common mistake* Failing to start all organizational planning by asking 'What are the aims?' Questions about what is the most efficient form of organization are meaningless unless this is done.

2. Is management trying to predict possible changes in its environment?

The rapid changes affecting many organizations, both public and private, mean that more effort needs to be spent on trying to understand and consider the implications for the organization of possible changes in the environment. Relevant changes for companies include those that affect its markets, whether they are actions by governments, actions by competitors, changes in consumer tastes or technical changes, those that affect its resources of money, staff and materials, and those that affect its freedom of action. Some adverse changes may be prevented or modified by good public relations.

Smaller companies are less likely to try to anticipate hostile changes in their environment. Many large companies have departments to do so as well as using forecasting centres and consultants. They can still get it wrong because the future even when it looks predictable may not be; for example, the predictions by at least one large oil company that supplies of oil would be nearing exhaustion before the end of the century. These predictions failed to take account of all the other factors that have proved relevant to the demands for oil.

- *Common mistake* Failing to recognize and to guard against potentially adverse changes in the environment.

3. Is the structure of the organization still appropriate?

The balance between order and flexibility and between centralization and decentralization may well need to change to meet changing conditions.

One of the specific questions to ask about the structure is whether the grouping of activities is still satisfactory (this was discussed in Chapter 3). It may often be necessary to review the location of particular activities. There may be many reasons for making changes. Technical changes, for example, may alter the economics of a central or a decentralized service as it has in computing and in institutional catering by the introduction of cook-chill. Other changes may point to using outside contractors or to taking the service closer to the clients.

- *Common mistake* Failing to recognize that the form of the organization no longer suits changed conditions.

4. Is the proposed organizational change really likely to be worth the upheaval that it will cause?

There is an opposite danger to the one above. It is that of being too keen to change the organizational structure. Structural change is often the one with the most appeal to top managers who may forget that all structures are a mix of advantages and disadvantages. The disadvantages of the present structure are clearly seen, together with the need to cope with hostile changes in the environment. But all too often the potential disadvantages of the new organization are not adequately considered, nor the certain costs of the dislocation during the change from one kind of structure to another.

- *Common mistake* Having a too optimistic view of the benefits of changes in organizational structure.

5. Are organizational policies still relevant to current conditions?

The rapid change that is affecting most organizations means that management should frequently review its policies to see if they are still appropriate. It is easy to lag behind; for example, to continue with the same recruitment and selection policies long after changes in the labour market and in social attitudes, or the need to recruit people with different abilities and attitudes, have made them inappropriate. Large organizations, especially, need to be alert to changes in the composition of the population and in education and social patterns, such as demographic changes in the number of young people, changes in the proportion of school-leavers going on to university, in the proportion of women working, in the average age of childbirth and in social attitudes to mobility.

- *Common mistake* Failing to review frequently the implications of all kinds of changes in the environment for organizational policies.

6. Which decisions are most vital to success? Who is taking these decisions?

Top management ought to determine which decisions are most important for success. These are the ones on which it should take the final decision. The danger is that top management will not have sought to identify the decisions that matter most, or that even if it has it will not spend the time necessary to give them adequate attention. One guide to the importance of a decision is an assessment of the repercussions of a mistake. For example, judging the timing and price for buying key raw materials is a vital aspect of some companies' profitability. In public service organizations the more important repercussions may be from mistakes that are likely to arouse public criticism. In a firm operating in a market of rapidly changing technology, failing to recognize and to react to the early signs of technical obsolescence can be a major mistake. In financial companies, especially, but in other companies too, failing to control adequately those who can rapidly lose the company a lot of money.

- *Common mistake* Management preoccupied with details and matters of secondary importance instead of concentrating on the most vital decisions. This is a danger at all management levels but it matters most at top management.

7. Which decisions should be taken by those who have to implement them?

There is much to be said for the view that decisions should be taken at the lowest level that is practicable. In Chapter 8, on decentralization, we saw some of the factors that affect what is practicable, and noted that these may vary at different stages of development. Many decisions are likely to be better if they are taken by those who know the local conditions and the people who will be affected. There are, of course, other decisions that will be better for the wider perspective that a more senior manager should be able to bring to the problem. Pushing decisions as far down the hierarchy as possible makes lower-level jobs more interesting. The implementation of decisions is also likely to be better, as people will usually be more motivated to carry out their own decisions than those of others.

Management may fail to decentralize because it has analysed neither the nature of the decisions nor where they ought to be taken. Often managers may take too many decisions themselves because they are reluctant to delegate.

- *Common mistake* Failing to realize which decisions are better taken at lower level, or reluctance to delegate.

8. (Looking at individual jobs) Why does this job exist? What is its holder supposed to contribute to the organization? What are the responsibilities?

Unless these questions are asked, jobs may be created that are unnecessary or, more commonly, may survive after the need has passed, as in the old story about the man who asked why there was a man in the gunnery team who apparently had nothing to do and was told 'Oh! He is there to hold the horses.'

It is particularly important to be clear about the purpose of a job, and the nature of its responsibilities, when deciding who would be suitable to appoint to it. Such clarity can also contribute to job satisfaction; most people feel happier if they know what it is they are supposed to be doing. Investigation may show that the duties of a particular job are seen quite differently by the holder, the boss, colleagues and subordinates. This may be due, at least in part, to a failure to define the purpose of the job.

- *Common mistake* Fuzzy thinking about the responsibilities of individual jobs.

9. (Looking at individual jobs) What is it like to be in this job? What are its strains, stresses and satisfactions?

Managers rarely think enough about what it is like to work in a particular job. They need to do so in order to understand how people may react to it and what the effect of these reactions will be on job performance. Research has taught us that quite different personalities may react in the same way to a particular job, and that reorganizing the job can change these reactions by modifying or removing conflicting demands. The aim should be to design jobs that people will be interested in doing well and which do not impose unnecessary physical or mental stress.

- *Common mistake* Thinking too little about what it is like to work in particular jobs and of the need to take this into account when designing jobs.

10. What effects does the form of organization have on people's relations with each other?

Research has shown us that one method of organization can create frictions and antagonisms between different individuals and groups, while another can encourage people to cooperate with each other. This is a lesson that is worth remembering wherever technology permits of alternative methods of work organization.

- *Common mistake* Failing to realize that the form of organization chosen can have repercussions on individual and group behaviour, and that these should be taken into account when considering the advantages and disadvantages of alternative methods of organizing work.

11. Are people in step with each other?

Organizations differ in the extent to which people cooperate with each other. They differ too in whether activities that must be related mesh smoothly together. Both are aspects of coordination, but deficiencies may stem either from a culture that has fostered a competitive rather than a cooperative culture or from poor organization and planning.

- *Common mistake* Failing to recognize symptoms of poor coordination or, if recognized to diagnose or tackle its causes.

12. What are the relations like between managerial and specialist staff?

Complaints of friction between operating managers and specialist departments are common, yet much can be done to encourage good working relations between the two groups. Organizational clarity in the relationship is important. What are the specialists supposed to do? Who do they report to? Are they there only to advise, or are there some areas where they are responsible for deciding what should be done? These questions should be asked and clearly answered. Important, too, are the attitudes of the two groups to each other. The specialist staff should see their role as that of professional advisers to clients. Management should learn how to draw on this professional knowledge without abdicating responsibility. The relationship is one that often improves with time as the two groups get more used to working with each other.

- *Common mistake* Poor relations between operating managers and specialists leading to inefficient use of specialist resources.

13. What are managerial relations like?

The effectiveness of an organization will depend, to a considerable extent, on the relations between individual managers. Do they work well together, or are they distracted by personal jealousies and power struggles? Some friction is likely and is probably healthy, but power struggles can be harmful to the pursuit of common objectives. The head of the organization should try to ensure that arguments are not conducted in a win-or-lose atmosphere.

- *Common mistake* Managers who pursue their sectional interests rather than identify with a common purpose.

14. Are people getting the information they need?

There are all too many ways in which communications can be unsatisfactory. There may be too much information, too little, or it may be of the wrong kind. Managers may be flooded with paper or Email which they have no time to read closely or even distinguish what matters and what does not. Managers may feel that their time is wasted in meetings that are too frequent and too lengthy. Alternatively, they may complain of having insufficient information about what is going on; that decisions are taken affecting them but about which they are not consulted, nor even told about. It is still worse where one receives the wrong kind of information – market analyses that are misleading, figures that are based on poor data or information that is deliberately selected so as to give too rosy a picture of what is happening.

Information often has to be passed from one person to another, or from one part of the organization to another. The official channels may be slow and inefficient; status differences may be a barrier to the free exchange of information. Additionally there are all the problems that arise from the fact that what I say may not be what you hear; the same thing may happen when you tell the next person, and so the information may get more distorted as it is passed on. The greater use of electronic information reduces some of the previous dangers, but it brings its own dangers too. Nor can it take the place of verbal communication when the nuances of words and behaviour need to be understood. There is a danger, particularly in the public sector, of overestimating the effectiveness of written communication for conveying changes in top management policies and for getting commitment to their implementation.

- *Common mistake* Too little attention given to what information is needed by whom and what is the most effective way of communicating it.

15. Is the organization's culture suitable for meeting current conditions?

An organization's culture is the distinctive ways in which employees behave and the assumptions that they share about the organization and its rationale. It will have developed to meet past circumstances and may no longer be appropriate for a changed environment. The importance of culture in helping to determine the effectiveness of an organization is well understood in some companies where considerable efforts are made to ensure that new entrants are selected to fit the organization and are taught the customary ways of thinking and acting. In such companies internal training will be used to foster an organizational culture and loyalty. In times of change there is a danger in such organizations that at least some of the cultural attitudes being inculcated may have become a source of weakness.

- *Common mistakes* In times of change, top management does not review the nature and relevance of the current organizational culture for meeting the challenges facing the organization. Even if it does, it fails to change its selection, appraisal, training, promotion and remuneration policies to try and develop a culture that is better suited to meeting the external challenges.

16. What thought is being given to management development and to career planning?

What experience should managers have and what is the best way for them to get it? These questions should be asked in all medium-sized and large organizations. The search for answers should range across the different kinds of management programmes, other forms of learning, such as membership of a project group or secondment to an external organization and the learning provided by particular jobs and job moves. The kind of experience that managers have will be partly determined by the form of organization. For example, young managers are likely to get more responsibility in decentralized organizations than in centralized ones.

The extent to which departments or subsidiaries are self-contained, each with its own career structure, will affect the opportunities that young men and women will have to get a wider view of the organization. The danger of departmental or occupational career ladders is that managers will tend to have a narrow viewpoint which can later be a handicap when they get to the top and have to view the organization as a whole. This danger is less than it was with the greater mobility across functions and between organizations.

- *Common mistake* Paying too little attention to career patterns and giving too little thought to the kind of experience that they provide.

There are in common mistakes 17 and 18 contrasting faults of over- and under-organization, both of which may exist in different parts of the same company.

17. Where is there too little systematization?

Many organizations, particularly those that have grown rapidly, have too little formalization. Policies are not defined, people do not know what they should be doing and too little effort has been given to trying to devise standardized ways of dealing with certain activities. The result is muddle and uncertainty.

- *Common mistake* Too little attention to trying to systematize the work to be done.

18. Where is there too much formalization and unnecessary red tape?

This is an appropriate mistake to have near the end because it is the popular idea of what is wrong with many large organizations. There is a tendency for those organizations that are already highly formalized to develop systems, forms and procedures merely for their own sake rather than for the purpose they should be serving. New committees or new procedures may be needed, but all too often the old ones are not reviewed to see if they still serve a useful purpose. Managers may become infatuated with orderliness, thus forgetting the value of flexibility.

- *Common mistake* An over-enthusiasm for trying to systematize the work to be done and the procedures to be followed, and a failure to review periodically the relevance of existing procedures.

19. What organizational changes are in fashion in the organization?

There tend to be fashions, even fads, with their own buzz words to describe the latest way of improving efficiency and enhancing commitment. Each may have its own value, whether it is quality circles, the 9/9 manager, profit-sharing, quality management or changing organizational culture. The danger is that they can too often be seen as a panacea for organizational ills and the difficulties of implementing them are underestimated.

- *Common mistake* Falling for the latest management fashion.

20. Do managers, particularly top managers, encourage a spirit of inquiry?

The adaptability that is now needed in most companies, and many public-sector and voluntary organizations too, requires a sensitivity to changes in the environment and an ability to learn. Hence the latest prescription for successful organizations: that their managers and professionals have to be continuously learning. This means an ability to acquire, and an alertness to, new knowledge; a willingness to examine and to learn from mistakes; and an acceptance of the need for good managers to be always learning.

- *Common mistake* Failing to encourage a spirit of inquiry.

Index